Shadow Woods and Ghosts Survey Guide

Christine Handley and Ian D. Rotherham with
Paul Ardron, Melvyn Jones, Barry Wright,
Andy Alder, Paul Smith and Ondrej Vild.

April 2013

The authors of the survey guide would like to thank all the volunteers who took part in the workshops, carried out field work and helped with the project. These included: Mike Bloy, Vince Boulter, Chris Brewster, Pauline Burnett, Frank Galbraith, Dave Gash, Thelma Griffiths, Averil Hudson, Deena Jeffreys, Jean Kendal, Stella Longden, Michael Parker, Paul Pugh, Brenda Roddis, Sheila Routledge, Chris Taylor, Dorothy Teague, Ava Teasdale, Clare Thompson, Jan Turner, Nick Wagg and Irene Wilkinson.

Written and edited by Christine Handley and Ian D. Rotherham with Paul Ardron, Melvyn Jones, Barry Wright, Andy Alder, Paul Smith and Ondrej Vild

ISBN 978-1-904098-51-5
Published by:
Wildtrack Publishing, Venture House,
103 Arundel Street, Sheffield S1 2NT

Typeset and processed by Christine Handley

Supported by:
BaLHRI.
Sheffield Hallam University.
HEC Associates Ltd.

With funding from:
Peak District National Park Authority's Sustainable Development Fund.
and
South Yorkshire Biodiversity Research Group.

Contents

Preface

Today, we see shadows and imprints of an ancient ecology in the modern landscape. Old meadows and pastures, ancient heaths, medieval coppice woods, and similar features bear testimony to this remarkable lineage. Ancient parks are the most visibly obvious remnants of formerly extensive grazed wooded landscapes. However, even where deer parks survive (and this is rare), they do so as unique landscapes separated in time and function from their origins. It may be that the greater medieval parks have shared common origins from the legacy of Vera's primeval savanna. However, other areas, upland moors and moorland fringe, and lowland heaths, commons and downs, probably reflect this same lineage; even today, many of these lands are grazed, and many have ancient albeit small, trees. These are the lands unenclosed in medieval times and linked, albeit tenuously, to Vera's open, fluid primeval landscape. For example, some of the species-rich grasslands such as the Derbyshire Dales limestone pastures are in effect, the remains of the open areas of Vera's landscape. Here are anciently complex, species-rich grasslands within landscapes of hazel and patches of ancient woodland (identified by Donald Pigott in the 1960s). These and other wooded sites are now being recognised as 'shadow woods' or 'ghosts woods'; either relicts from once obviously ancient woodland sites, or perhaps more excitingly, ancient wooded landscapes until now overlooked.

Parks are the most obvious landscapes that mix trees and grazing animals. However, once one starts to examine the landscape more critically, it is apparent that many other systems have a similar approach. Heaths, commons, and unenclosed pastures (like Longshaw, North Derbyshire), mix ancient trees and open grazing lawns with long-term continuity of management to match that of the nearby Chatsworth Park. A major difference is that ancient trees in these landscapes are generally small and may be species such as hawthorns, which are often overlooked. Examining ecology and soils in these wider landscapes reveals the imprint or 'shadow' of former 'woodland' status; they are 'ancient wooded landscapes'.

English wooded landscapes result from millennia of human interaction with nature. Their early beginnings were as various forms of pasture woods, and originally an expansive patchwork landscape of forest, wetland, grassland and other naturally occurring 'habitats' with large grazing herbivores. The descendants of these original ecosystems and landscapes persist today as woods and other 'unimproved' landscape features, and as 'shadows' and 'ghosts'. In this context, a new and emerging challenge for our research concepts and paradigms is to step outside the boundary of the medieval 'woods' in search of the shadows, ghosts, and footprints of a wider wooded landscape. In particular, the recognition of 'grazed wooded landscapes', and of 'shadow woods', is especially significant. Indeed, the recent recognition of the wider resource of ancient wooded landscapes has provided further impetus for such studies.

The idea or concept of 'Ghost' or 'Shadow' woods, as I have called them, came from thirty years or more of field survey and historical research into woodlands, heaths, moors, bogs and fens. Along with the concepts of the 'eco-cultural nature of landscapes' and of 'cultural severance', this begins to unify our vision of landscape yesterday, today, and tomorrow. The ghosts are there in moors, heaths and grasslands, from extensive grazed 'woods' to tiny pockets of roadside verge. You have only to look.

Ian D. Rotherham, 2013

Introduction

The '*Shadow Woods and Ghosts*' survey guide has been produced by SYBRG (South Yorkshire Econet) with funding from the Peak District National Park Authority's Sustainable Development Fund as part of the '*Looking for the Ghosts & Shadows of Woodlands Past*' project. This project set out to uncover the hidden woodland past around the eastern fringes of the Peak District and western edge of the Sheffield conurbation. The main study area roughly equates to the Sheffield Moors Partnership Area.

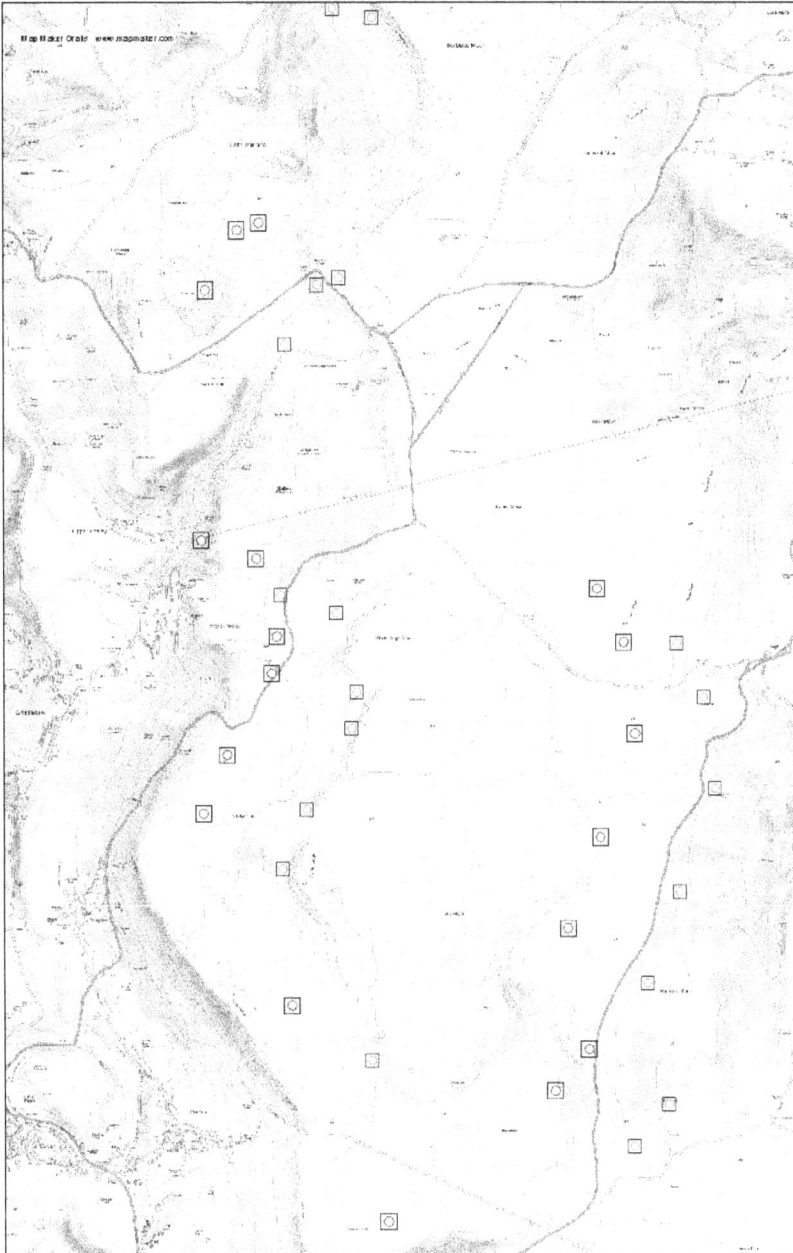

Shadow Woods & Ghosts Core Project Area 2012

THE SURVEY GUIDE

The survey guide is based on material produced from the *Woodland Heritage Champions* project and more recent research looking at how woodlands may persist in the landscape. Additional material has been contributed by local volunteers who have taken part in a series of '*Shadow Woods and Ghosts*' workshops around the eastern fringe of the Peak District.

Topics covered by the workshops and included in this survey guide are introductions to:

- investigating the forms and management of trees and shrubs and how these reflect their past uses and the history of a tree'd landscape (treescape).
- investigating surface archaeological features such as pits, platforms, boundary banks and routeways.
- recording and understanding botanical indicators of woodland.
- using archival and other material to investigate the history of tree'd landscapes.
- carrying out surveys of woodland features and using archival material to inform and interpret the survey data.

The guide is designed so that it can be used by local volunteers and interested professionals who haven't attended the workshops. The guide is specifically designed for use in the eastern Peak District, but will also be of great interest to those elsewhere in the country. Section 1 sets out the basic techniques for fieldwork and contains survey forms for collecting information. Section 2 gives background information and a general understanding of upland treescapes, shadows and ghosts. Section 3 looks at collating data from the surveys and using this to inform management and create a permananent record from the findings. The final two sections give supporting information and suggestions for further reading.

An upland veteran Rowan. Is this a Shadow or a Ghost?
© Ian Rotherham

1. Investigating the Landscape: Using Documentary Evidence and Reminiscences.

INTRODUCTION

Most ancient woods and other wooded landscapes such as deer parks and wooded commons have some form of documented history. Such sites were of economic importance to their owners and their management histories have often survived in great detail over long periods of time. The documentary record which may describe past conditions, past events and past management practices may be less obvious in relation to some of the 'shadows' and 'ghosts' under investigation. In these cases there may be fewer direct sources of evidence as the treescapes either occured on less productive land or their use was governed by 'custom & practice' at a domestic / farm level. Here some of the indirect sources of evidence or, for more recent times, personal reminiscences may reveal the existence and uses of these treescapes.

DOCUMENTARY EVIDENCE

Documentary evidence can, for example, provide accurate details about the tree composition of a wood at particular dates, about when planting was done and what tree species were planted, about when a wood was extended or reduced in size, about how coppicing was organised and when coppice management ceased, and about the markets for the wood and timber. Details are also often provided about grazing regimes, the construction and maintenance of boundary banks and walls, the preparation of charcoal hearths, the digging and filling in of saw pits, quarrying and mining activity. For most woods, the documentary evidence will not be continuous and will be more plentiful for the post-medieval period. Nevertheless, using ecological and archaeological evidence alone can make it much harder to be sure of past conditions, events and the management practices which were carried out, exactly when and for how long.

TYPES OF EVIDENCE

The types of documentary evidence can be extremely varied from detailed estate accounts, leases and maps, manorial court records to newspaper cuttings, photographs, diaries and ephemera. They can be direct forms of evidence related to the management of a particular treescape, for example an estate account book giving the numbers and types of trees felled or planted. Or, the evidence can be indirect,

Some of the Main Types of Evidence	
Type	**Description and Comments**
Maps / Plans	Variable scales, sizes and subjects prior to Ordnance Survey
Place Names	Often reflects earliest occupancy and use but may be modern
Photographs / Paintings / Sketches	Information is often found in the background or is incidental
Estate Plans/ Accounts/ Surveys	May provide extremely detailed information on management
Enclosure Awards / Tithe Awards	Identifies all parcels of land and ownership at specific date
Manorial Records / Court Rolls	Administrative and legal records relating to specific areas
Parish Records	Records relating to rating of properties as well as registers
County Reports / Victoria County Histories	Good overall background source if available
Newspapers / Journals / Trade Directories	Specific information about commercial development
National Surveys and Inventories	Can give details for local area and set information in context
Diaries / Recollections / Interviews	Provides individual and sometimes 'hidden' information

for example a survey for a turnpike road which notes areas of woodland, their size and ownership. It is important when using any type of evidence, especially at first, to make an assessment of how apt it is for the questions you need answering. The documents were produced at a particular time, for a particular purpose and even if this is directly related to a particular treescape the meaning of the language used may have changed. Wherever possible more than one type of evidence should be used to corroborate the information.

SOURCES OF EVIDENCE

Sources for documentary evidence range from official government departments to collections of documents kept by individuals in their own homes. Access to the former is governed by agreed protocols, for the latter, it is often the case that their existence is revealed accidentally. The growth of the use of the internet through expansion of websites and schemes to make information publicly available means that searching for documentary evidence is much easier than in the past if you have access to the internet. Many individual maps, documents, recordings and photographs are also available directly from this source so some preliminary work can be carried out locally no matter where the original documents are kept. Coverage however is likely to be patchy at best so as with types of evidence it is best to visit different sources to get a comprehensive picture.

Some of the Main Sources of Evidence	
Type	**Description and Comments**
Internet / websites	Need to be aware of the accuracy, authority, objectivity, currency and coverage of websites. A recent book *Internet Sites for Local Historians* had 518 entries when published.
Historic Environment Records / Sites and Monuments Records	Includes records of archaeological sites as well as finds, events and reports for an area plus maps, plans and associated publications. Useful as a starting point to find out what is already known for your area. Information is held by the County Council, the National Park Authority. The National Trust has its own HER for its land holdings.
Public Libraries: Local Studies / Reference	Widely based collections of published information eg. newspapers, trade directories, pamphlets, local histories of an area as well as maps and census records.
Archives & County Records Offices	Official repositories for legal & administrative records from public bodies including churches, schools and local councils as well as private companies and estates.
Local Authority Planning Departments	They may have management or conservation area plans which include historical, archaeological and ecological information.
Landowners	Some landowners still maintain estate records eg. at Chatsworth; others have deposited historical records at an archive or record office. Landowners may also be public bodies and have current management information available.
Local History Societies, Archeaology and Natural History Groups	May have direct information about treescapes or other information and contacts which will lead to direct information. Potential good source of local knowledge not available elsewhere.
Local people	Individual or family related both direct and indirect.

REMINISCENCES

These include autobiographies, diaries and journals written years ago as well as contemporary recordings and writing. Although some of the memories will be selective, written for a particular purpose, guided by an interviewer or with a view to publication they can nevertheless uncover information about treescapes and the part they played in the every day lives of people. These reminiscences often give insights into particular ways that people worked or used the treescapes which are no longer carried out. Recording these memories through a community oral history project is a separate project outside the scope of this guide. It can be resource intensive but very rewarding.

Lunchtime discussion © SYBRG 2012

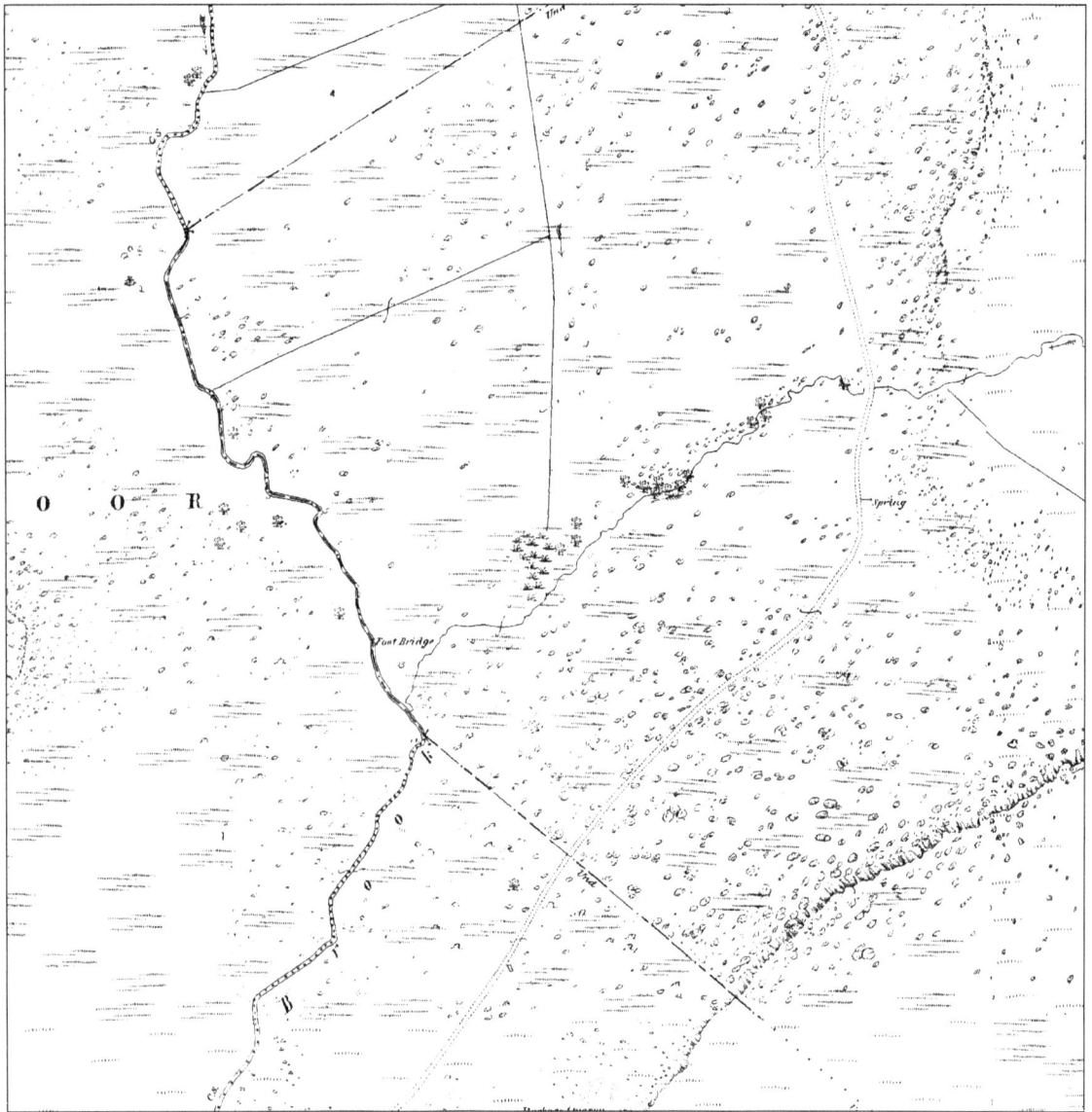

First Edition Ordnance Survey Map (mid-nineteenth century) Showing Part of Upper Burbage Moor with Trees, Boulder Scatter, Field Boundaries and Area of Bog.

1. *Investigating the Landscape: Maps and Mapping*

INTRODUCTION

Maps can be a very useful source of information to identify areas of woodland, changes to boundaries and associated place-names starting with modern maps and working backwards to the earliest maps for the area. The project area is already covered by reports using series of maps which gives detailed background infornmaton for survey work.

Maps are also essential for recording features including trees as part of survey work especially when linked to the Ordnance Survey grid reference system. Making such a record enables the location of a feature to be fixed so that others can re-visit it in the future, especially important if management is taking place on a site.

HISTORIC MAPS

These are a type of documentary evidence which can provide often very detailed information about changes in treescapes both pictorially and by using place-name evidence when a sequence of maps are examined. From the nineteenth century onwards the Ordnance Survey have produced standardised maps across the country at various scales. The first edition of the detailed 25-inch to the mile (1:2,500) series was produced in the 1890s for the local area and details individual trees along boundaries and in non-woodland areas as well as giving the boundaries of woods. Comparing these areas with woodland coverage shown on modern maps will help to show potential sites for 'shadows' and 'ghosts'. Prior to Ordnance Survey, maps were commissioned by landowners

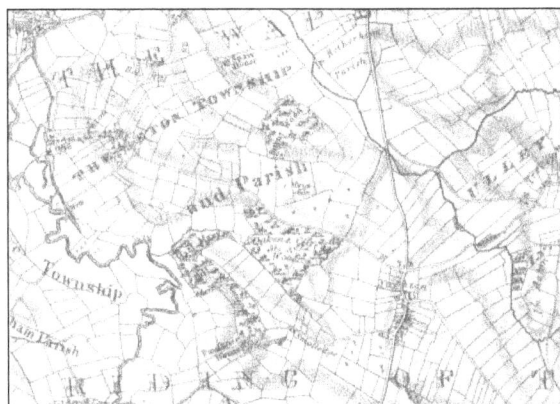

Extract from Sanderson's Map 'Twenty Miles around Mansfield' (1835).

who needed detailed plans of their estates or, especially from the late eighteenth century, produced commercially for different audiences. Some of these maps are detailed whilst others give partial or pictorial information which cannot be located accurately. Maps were also produced as part of land surveys such as for Enclosure Awards and may have accompanying note books which give more detail about land ownership and use which is useful for looking at the continuity of treescapes.

THE LOCAL RESOURCE

Much of the land within the core project area has already had archaeological surveys organised by the Peak District National Park Authority and the National Trust/RSPB. The survey reports include plans of all the known features supported by a detailed gazeteer which gives descriptions and interpretations of each feature recorded. Copies of the surveys are held by the National Park Authority and the National Trust / RSPB. It is recommended that the survey reports are consulted at an early stage of research into *Shadows and Ghost woods* as they will greatly assist in recognising and interpreting associated archaeological sites. The surveys can be consulted by appointment with the National Park's Cultural Heritage Team.

At a more general level, an Historic Landscape Character report has been produced by the Peak District National Park Authority. This covers the whole of the Authority's area and gives an analysis of how the current landscape has developed over time. It includes information on all the available early maps and historical surveys and is another very useful source of background information for surveying *Shadows and Ghosts*. A copy of the report can also be consulted via the National Park's Cultural Heritage Team.

Most of the core project area is also covered by the Sheffield Moors Partnership and / or Eastern Moors Partnership both of which have produced reports available on their websites which have maps of the area giving useful background information about features and sites.

MODERN MAPS

It is now possible to order an Ordnance Survey map which has your study area at the centre on-line (via a mapping website) either as digital version or as a paper copy. Low-cost and in some cases free software is also available from websites to allow you to make a map of your survey results and superimpose it onto a base map or aerial photograph. These together with the use of GPS for recording and with in-built maps for locating features enables volunteers to create quite sophisticated maps. These can be updated with new survey information and can be used to analyse and interpret the data from several different sources. If you are interested in undertaking detailed work in this way there are several entries listed in the bibliography to follow up.

Using a series of maps and recording survey information on base maps as described above can still be carried out, if more laboriously, as a paper and acetate sheet exercise. The principle of using a base map at a certain scale (we recommend 1:2,500) recording archaeological and ecological features at the same scale and superimposing them over each other is still relevant. In the case of 'shadows' and 'ghosts' it may reveal sites which look recent but are much older and vice versa. More information about using maps in a practical way is given in the survey section.

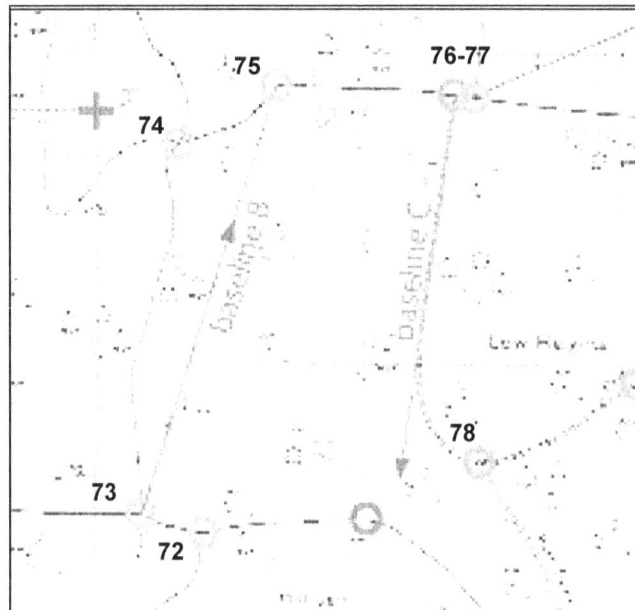

Extract from Woodland Survey Map Showing the Plotting of Features. © SYBRG 2008

1. Investigating the Landscape: Undertaking Surveys

PREPARATION
There are a few simple stages to consider before you or members of your group undertake a field survey. The first, which may seem obvious, is to use an Ordnance Survey map to identify a discrete area to survey which is manageable, for example, along the bottom of Whites Edge. This will help focus activity and direct any documentary research.

PERMISSION
Much of the survey area is on open-access land. Nevertheless, where appropriate, ensure you have permission to carry out the survey and be aware of any restrictions during the lambing, bird-breeding or grouse shooting seasons. Contact with the landowner to let them know what you intend to do, where and when is needed in some areas. You may need to re-assure the landowners that you are not planning to do any excavation type work or harm trees and other vegetation. They will also be able to tell you whether there is any management operation (e.g thinning trees) being carried out which may affect your survey. Always offer to let them have a copy of your survey results. They may also have copies of other information which may be useful for your historical work that they will allow you to see.

HEALTH AND SAFETY ADVICE
Before you start your surveys, please read the points below carefully.
- The East Peak core project area, as with other areas of the Peak District, has been extensively mined and quarried for hundreds of years. This has left a legacy of old quarry pits, bellpits, adits and shafts of various sizes across the area which may still pose a danger. They may be covered in vegetation or appear stable but are not so extreme caution is needed when surveying areas where these features are present. The landowner should be able to tell you whether there are quarrying and mining features in your survey area. Previous surveys and old maps should also be consulted.
- If you are part of a community group you may be insured; however, you need to check before carrying out any survey. If your group does have insurance you should fill out a RISK ASSESSMENT and check what guidelines apply. If your group does not have insurance or you do not belong to a group please be aware that you are carrying out all survey work AT YOUR OWN RISK.
- Carry out all survey work with other group members or a friend, do not work alone. Make sure you carry a mobile phone and emergency numbers and leave details of your mobile phone number, route/location and expected return time with a friend or family member.
- Carry a first aid kit, sufficient drink and food, and any personal medication that you require. It is recommended that at least one of your group has up-to-date first aid training.
- Ensure you have permission to carry out a survey (see previous section). Always let the landowner(s) know a few days beforehand when and where you will be on site.
- The ground in upland areas and woodlands can be uneven and there are likely to be trip hazards such as boulders, fallen branches, ditches and exposed roots. It may also be cold and wet. Wear sturdy footwear and suitable clothing for the weather conditions.
- Do not carry out surveys during adverse weather conditions particularly storms, high winds and heavy snow fall.

Please make sure that you are properly prepared for your visit. It is your responsibility to take care of your own safety and that you follow the up-to-date health and safety guidelines for your group.

BASIC FIELD EQUIPMENT

Listed below are items needed to carry out field surveys. Some are optional and you will not need all of these for each survey.

- Maps: We recommend that you carry out all your field surveys at a scale of 1:2,500 (1mm on your plan = 2.5m on the ground). This scale will correspond to the largest scale maps produced by the Ordnance Survey.
- Notebook and pencil: Waterproof notebooks can be bought in many outdoor shops and pencils are more effective in damp conditions than pens. Make sure you also take a pencil sharpener and eraser.
- Ruler for measuring distances on the map (preferably with mapping scales including 1:2,500). A set-square may also be useful for plotting points on a map.
- Tape Measure: at least one but preferably three: 30m or 50m; these can be used as a guide for setting up transects as well as measuring individual features or girths of trees.
- Hand-held GPS: not essential but useful especially now the up-to-date ones work better under woodland canopies. Practise using this in advance including downloading information from the unit to your computer. It is advisable still to keep a paper record of your plots - just in case!
- Compass and 360-degree protractor (if no GPS so you can plot points on your map accurately) .
- Camera: preferably a digital one
- Sticks (Bamboo Canes) and Hazard Tape: to mark features to return to or as scale guides when photographing features.
- Torch: useful for examining hollow trees and building interiors (if safe to do so).
- Identification Guides: for tree, wildlife and vegetation surveys.
- Mobile phones (check mobile phone reception) or Two-way radios: for communication if your group splits up, as well as for emergencies.
- Small (personal) First Aid Kit if you do not have a designated First-aider in your survey team.

More guidance is given in publications listed in the bibliography

Looking for Twayblade (Neottia ovata) on Blackamoor, June 2012 © SYBRG

1. Investigating the Landscape: Recording landscape features: general survey

INTRODUCTION

As a starting point, even if you already know the area well, it is often useful to carry out a rapid but thorough reconnaissance visit / walk-over survey. This will help to set the treescape and any features you find there into their landscape context and may be done before any documentary research. The aim of this initial walk-over survey is to acquire an overview of your study area: its geology, topography, ecology and most obvious historic features. At this stage do not spend too long examining any individual tree, patch of ground flora or potential archaeological feature. The walk-over (general) survey form can be completed supplemented with photographs or with a few sketches on your map or in your notebook. This basic information will help you to structure any more detailed surveys and target areas for particular investigation.

A survey of a large area can seem daunting so it is easier break it down systematically into smaller, more manageable chunks, and agree a suitable timetable to complete coverage of the whole area. Check that the area is not already divided into compartments which is often the case if management / farming operations are carried out. If compartments already exist then it may be more meaningful if your surveys match these. It is recommended that a general survey (Level 1) of the whole study area is carried out before a very detailed survey of a smaller area otherwise potentially unique features may be overlooked. Always remember that, as a volunteer, you can return to the woodland and expand the surveys at a later date.

Minimum Dataset:

As a minimum all surveys need to include the following information:
The date of the survey; who carried out the survey; where the survey was carried out (provide map references or GPS reference points where possible); what features were found and a description or take pictures / make a sketch of any feature you feel is significant.

Maps:

An appropriate map and the skills to locate and record features onto a base map, is key to undertaking survey work. The 1:2,500 scale (1mm on the map = 2.5m on the ground) map is recommended for the general survey. It will have fixed point features already mapped which you can locate, check that they still exist and then use them as reference points for your more detailed mapping and to orientate yourself.

SURVEY FORM (LEVEL 1 SURVEY)

A 2-page general survey form is included in this pack. The form has been designed to help gather information about the landscape context and record obvious features which may need further survey. Once complete it should provide a good summary of your survey area.

Page 1:

Section 1 asks for basic details of surveyor(s), date, and general location. including an average height above sea level (asl). This may be important in later interpretation of features and presence of trees.

Section 2 asks for a central grid reference and approximate area under survey; this information can be taken from the base map. If your survey area is long and thin, grid references for the two ends can be given. This section also asks you to note the surrounding topography, aspect and slope. If the topography etc varies over the survey area then record the changes and include a grid reference of the change.

Section 3 should be used to record the main habitat types found within the survey area. Distinct areas may form part of a later detailed survey later but for this stage an overall assessment is sufficient. As a general guide when surveying woodlands we suggest that you follow all the major footpaths and note down any distinctive features you can see from them. In a more open moorland situation observations from walking a single footpath may be sufficient. The sort of features you are looking for include, any large, tightly clustered or misshapen trees or shrubs; distinct patches of ground flora; changes in vegetation; square, oblong, oval platforms; round, oval or oblong hollows or pits; entrances or gateways; tracks or paths; any streams, watercourses, boggy or flush area; and any standing building / structural remains, ditches, banks, fences, walls or large boulders.

Section 4 should be used to summarise the features you have listed on page two of the form and gives space for you to note anything which appears striking or instances where features overlay one another.

Page 2:
The main section, Section 5, on the second page is set out as a table to allow you to record the position of individual features with a brief description (using the keywords from sections 4 and 6 on the form) and whether you have taken a photograph. It will be helpful for later work to note down any features, numbering them in sequence, onto your base survey map of the area as well as the survey form or in a notebook with a brief description. You need to include a grid reference or GPS location for each feature. A grid reference is essential so that you and other people can locate the feature in the future. Grid references can be derived either directly from an Ordnance Survey map or using a hand-held Global Positioning System (GPS). A continuation sheet with the table format is included in the survey pack.

Section 6 should be used to summarise the features found in the survey, to enable you to assess the data you collect and pinpoint where you will need to carry out more detailed work. It can act as a useful summary for other people especially if a group is involved in a larger survey or with different aspects of the work.

1. Investigating the Landscape: General Walk-over Survey

1. GENERAL INFORMATION

Site Name		Surveyor(s) Name(s)	
Site Location (description)		Altitude (metres asl)	Date of Survey

2. TREE'D LANDSCAPE LOCATION AND SITUATION

Grid Reference (Centre using map)		Approx. size (in hectares)		
Topography of the landscape (Situation of the tree'd area)	Broad valley Narrow valley Plain Hill Plateau Lowland Moorland Crag/cliff Other (describe)			
Slope (Is the site located on a slope and is this uniform throughout)	Vertical Steep Undulating Gently Sloping Flat			
Aspect (if the site is located on a slope)	North East South West			

3. TREE'D LANDSCAPE OVERALL HABITAT TYPE (circle all that apply)

Upland Wood Pasture / Moorland Edge	Boulder Slope - Medusoid trees
Carr (Wet) Woodland	Clough woodlands (steep valley sides)
Parkland (wood pasture)	Isolated stunted trees / moorland trees
Broadleaved woodland - dominant	Wet boggy area
Conifer woodland - dominant	Roadside verge
Other (specify) / Notes	

4. FEATURES IN THE TREE'D LANDSCAPE (circle all that apply)

Grazed areas	Disturbed / bare ground	Marshy / boggy areas
Springs / streams / flushes	Ponds / standing water	Ditches / goits / culverts
Stone walls	Bank(s)	Routeways / paths / trackways
Standing dead wood	Rock Exposure	Platform(s)
Dead wood on ground	Moorland	Pits / Hollows
Specify Other / Notes		

5. SUMMARY OF FEATURES FOUND IN THE TREE'D LANDSCAPE. NOTE: RECORD THE FEATURE NUMBER ON YOUR BASE MAP **WHILST CARRYING OUT THE SURVEY** (use continuation pages for your survey if needed)

Feature Number	Grid Reference (s)	Description / Notes	Photograph / sketch (yes/number)

6. SUMMARY DESCRIPTION /INFERENCES / INTERPRETATION

Description keywords (circle all that apply)	Pit Platform Mound Earthfast stone / post Pile of Stones Standing building Ruined building Other Structure Bank Ditch/ channel Fence /wall Route / trackway Tree-throw pits Ancient / Veteran / Worked tree(s) Pasture Wood Plantation Hedge. Other (specify)
Description of features and inferences	
Interpretation	
Further survey work / research required	Yes / No / Not Sure

5. SUMMARY OF FEATURES FOUND IN THE TREE'D LANDSCAPE. NOTE: RECORD THE FEATURE NUMBER ON YOUR BASE MAP **WHILST CARRYING OUT THE SURVEY** (continuation sheet if needed)

Feature Number	Grid Reference (s)	Description / Notes	Photograph / sketch (yes/number)

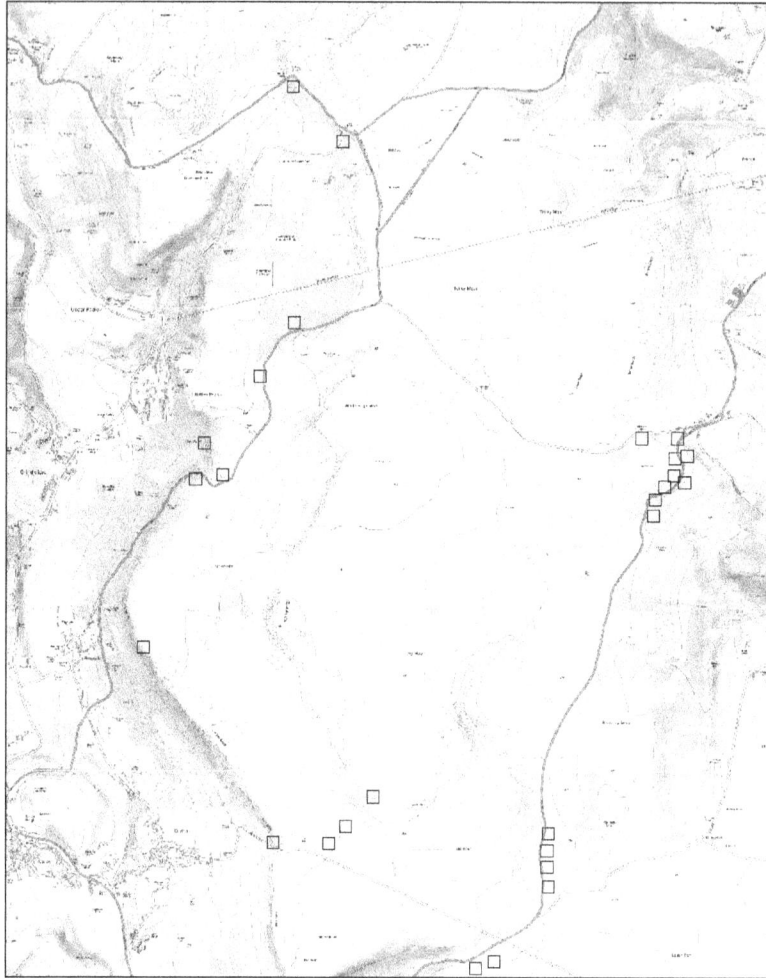

Recording Botanical Indicators: Location of Bluebell (Hyacinthoides non scripta) records from 2012 Project Survey. [blue squares]

1. *Investigating the Landscape: Recording Botanical Indicators*

INTRODUCTION

Ideally this survey should be undertaken after an initial walk-over survey which has recorded potential archaeology, worked trees and natural features. This can then be used to pinpoint areas for botanical surveys. The optimum time for botanical surveys for woodland species is late spring / early summer although many of the species will persist for longer some may not and others will become hidden by other vegetation such as bracken. You should be aware of this when undertaking the survey especially if you are not familiar with some of the species. The aim of the botanical indicators survey is to record the presence of species which may be associated with woodland growing conditions. The survey form does not give a comprehensive list of species which may occur in the survey area. If you want to create a complete species list you can use the form as a base. The survey is designed to collect a large amount of information in a summary form quite quickly to enable you to assess whether the area you are surveying has had a past woodland history. This basic information can then be used with other survey and documentary research to interpret the landscape.

As with the walk-over survey, a large area can seem daunting so again it is easier to break it down systematically into smaller, more manageable chunks, and agree a suitable timetable to complete coverage of the whole area. Use the same compartments as the ones in your walk-over so that information from different sources can be compared. Indicator plants such as Bluebell may also be found on places such as roadside verges. This may be the first indication of a ghost wood.

Minimum Dataset:

As a minimum all surveys need to include the following information:
The date of the survey (this is especially important for the botanical survey because time of year can affect the species found); who carried out the survey; where the survey was carried out (provide map references or GPS reference points where possible); and the species found.

Maps:

An appropriate map is needed, preferrably at the same scale as the walk-over survey. The 1:2,500 scale (1mm on the map = 2.5m on the ground) map is recommended for general use. It will have fixed point features already mapped ie a road or boundary which you can then use as reference points for your more detailed mapping and to orientate yourself.

SURVEY FORM (BOTANICAL INDICATORS)

A 4-page survey form is included in this pack. The form has been designed to help gather information about the landscape context and record the occurrence and estimated abundance of woodland species in a concise manner. The species on the form are grouped according to how strongly they can be defined as an ancient woodland indicator in this (Peak District) area of the UK. The species whether tree, herb, grass or fern are listed in alphabetical common name order again for ease of use locally.

Page 1:

The sections on this page ask for the same information from page 1 of the general survey and if appropriate the information can be transferred from there. However if you are carrying out the botanical indicators survey on a smaller area, fill in the details on page 1 JUST for the smaller area to give a detailed picture of the topography etc.

Section 1 asks for basic details of surveyor(s), date, and general location. including an average height above sea level (asl). This may be important in later interpretation of features and presence of trees.

Section 2 asks for a central grid reference and approximate area under survey; this information can be taken from the base map. If your survey area is long and thin, grid references for the two ends can be given. This section also asks you to note the surrounding topography, aspect and slope. If the topography etc varies over the survey area then record the changes and include a grid reference of the change.

Section 3 should be used to record the main habitat types found within the survey area. Try to record all the distinct types; the sort of features you are looking for include, any large, tightly clustered or misshapen trees or shrubs; distinct patches of ground flora and changes in vegetation; and any streams, watercourses, boggy or flush areas with different vegetation.

Section 4 should be used to record any distinct features which may affect the presence of botanical indicators or appears striking. The notes section can be used to record instances where features overlay one another.

Pages 2 to 4:

Basic information about using the survey forms to record species is given in the key and guidance at the top of page 2. The form is designed to be used for three levels of survey. The most basic is a record of presence of a species and for this a tick can be made in the O column on the sheet. If you want to record overall abundance of a species across the survey area then column L should be used togerher with the grading system described in the key. Where there are particularly interesting places (abundance of a range of species) or distinct habitat-types within the survey area a standing quadrat survey can be undertaken. Here the surveyor chooses a reference point to stand at within the habitat and surveys in a 2metre x 360° sweep from where s/he is standing recording all the species found and making a note of the grid reference (GR) of the reference point. It may be useful to take several copies of the survey form with you in case you find you want to do more than 5 standing quadrats.

It is possible to build up a detailed picture quite readily by using the three levels of survey. But if time is limited recording the presence of a species at a basic level will also produce useful information. You will probably need to use all three pages to record the species you find and there is also space to record any additional species of interest.

A list of the main field identification guides and sources of information is given in the bibliography. There are also some guides and keys now available on-line for use with smart phones etc.

1. *Investigating the Landscape: Botanical Indicators Survey Form*

1. GENERAL INFORMATION

Site Name		Surveyor(s) Name(s)	
Site Location / Altitude (metres asl)		Date of Survey	

2. TREE'D LANDSCAPE LOCATION AND SITUATION

Grid Reference (Centre using map)		Approx. size (in hectares)		
Topography of the landscape (Situation of the tree'd area)	Broad valley Narrow valley Plain Hill Plateau Lowland Moorland Crag/cliff Other (describe)			
Slope (Is the site located on a slope and is this uniform throughout)	Vertical Steep Undulating Gently Sloping Flat			
Aspect (if the site is located on a slope)	North East South West			

3. TREE'D LANDSCAPE OVERALL HABITAT (circle all that apply)

Upland Wood Pasture / Moorland Edge	Boulder Slope - Medusoid trees
Carr (Wet) Woodland	Clough woodlands (steep valley sides)
Parkland (wood pasture)	Isolated stunted trees / moorland trees
Broadleaved woodland - dominant	Wet boggy area
Conifer woodland - dominant	Roadside verge
Other (specify) / Notes	

4. FEATURES IN THE TREE'D LANDSCAPE (circle all that apply)

Grazed areas	Disturbed / bare ground	Marshy / boggy areas
Springs / streams / flushes	Ponds / standing water	Ditches / goits / culverts
Stone walls	Bank(s)	Routeways / paths / trackways
Standing dead wood	Rock Exposure	Platform(s)
Dead wood on ground	Moorland	Pits / Hollows
Specify Other / Notes		

Key.

Species marked with an asterisk (*) are the key species for identification. Species are grouped according to subjective categories based on observations in the local Peak District area and may vary if work is carried out in other areas of the UK. Species are listed in broadly alphabetical common name order.

An indication of tree species can be recorded here but any trees which you consider to be noteworthy / significant should also be recorded separately using the veteran / worked trees recording sheet (see later in pack)

The recording sheet has been devised to allow you to record presence of species using the Double DAFOR system (DDAFOR) using columns O and L. There is also space for up to five standing quadrats to be recorded (columns 1 to 5). If time is limited or you simply want to record overall presence of a species please use column O. *A description of the DDAFOR system is given in the background notes.*

For ease of recording a 'Spidergram' system can be used, as, follows:

/ Rare (<=5%)	✕ Occasional (6-19%)	✕| Frequent (20-45%)	✕⧗ Abundant (46-75%)	⧗✕⧗ Dominant (76% +)

A space is also given to the right of the form for you to record whether photographs or supplementary information was taken at the time of the survey.

A. Strong Ancient Woodland Indicators

Common Name	Scientific Name	O	L	1	2	3	4	5	Note(s) / photos.
Alder*	*Alnus glutinosa*								
Ancient Hawthorn*	*Crataegus monogyna*								
Ancient Hazel*	*Corylus avellana*								
Ancient Holly*	*Ilex aquifolium*								
Climbing Corydalis*	*Ceratocapnus claviculata*								
Common Bluebell*	*Hyacinthoides non scripta*								
Common Cow-wheat*	*Melampyrum pratense*								
Creeping Soft-grass*	*Holcus mollis*								
Dog's Mercury*	*Mercurialis perennis*								
Golden Saxifrage	*Chrysosplenium oppositifolia*								
Greater Stitchwort*	*Stellaria holostea*								
Greater Wood-rush	*Luzula sylvatica*								
Hairy Wood-rush	*Luzula pilosa*								
Honeysuckle	*Lonicera periclymenum*								
Lesser Skullcap	*Scutellaria minor*								
Oak sp.*	*Quercus sp*								
Smooth-stalked Sedge	*Carex laevigata*								
Wavy Hair-grass*	*Deschampsia flexuosa*								
Wild Garlic	*Allium ursinum*								
Wood Horsetail	*Equisetum sylvaticum*								
Wood Sage*	*Teucrium scorodonia*								
Wood Sorrel*	*Oxalis corniculata*								
Yellow Pimpernel	*Lysimachia nemorum*								

B. Good Ancient Woodland Indicators

Common Name	Scientific Name	O	L	1	2	3	4	5	Note(s)/ Photo.
Ancient Birch*	*Betula spp.*								
Ancient Rowan*	*Sorbus aucuparia*								
Angelica	*Angelica sylvestris*								
Aspen	*Populus tremula*								
Barren Strawberry	*Potentilla sterilis*								
Bird Cherry	*Prunus padus*								
Broad Buckler fern	*Dryopteris dilatata*								
Chickweed Wintergreen	*Trientalis europaea*								
Devil's-bit Scabious	*Succisa pratensis*								
Golden-scaled Male Fern	*Dryopteris affinis*								
Greater Tussock Sedge	*Carex paniculata*								
Green-ribbed Sedge	*Carex binervis*								
Hard Fern	*Polystichum aculeatum*								
Hart's-tongue Fern	*Phyllitis scolopendrium*								
Pignut	*Conopodium majus*								
Pill Sedge	*Carex pilulifera*								
Red Campion	*Silene dioica*								
Remote Sedge	*Carex remota*								
Tufted Hair-grass	*Deschampsia caespitosa*								
Wild Raspberry	*Rubus idaeus*								
Wild Strawberry	*Fragaria vesca*								
Woody Nightshade	*Solanum dulcamara*								

C. Woodland Indicators

Common Name	Scientific Name	O	L	1	2	3	4	5	Note(s) / Photo.
Bay Willow	*Salix pentandra*								
Common Dog Violet	*Viola riviniana*								
Crab Apple	*Malus sylvestris*								
Eared Willow	*Salix aurita*								
Grey Willow	*Salix cinerea*								
Lesser Celandine	*Ranunculus ficaria*								
Three-veined Sandwort	*Moehringia trinervia*								
Wood Avens	*Geum urbanum*								

D. Possible Indicators

Common Name	Scientific Name	O	L	1	2	3	4	5	Note(s) / Photo.
Bramble	*Rubus fruticosus*								
Common Bilberry	*Vaccinium myrtillus*								
Cowberry	*Vaccinium vitis-idaea*								
Goat Willow	*Salix caprea*								
Marsh Marigold	*Caltha palustris*								
Spindle	*Euonymus europaea*								

E. Associate Species

Common Name	Scientific Name	O	L	1	2	3	4	5	Note(s) / Photo.
Ancient Bracken Stands	*Pteridium aquilinum*								
Bog Asphodel	*Narthecium ossifragum*								
Dog Rose	*Rosa canina*								
Field Rose	*Rosa arvensis*								
Foxglove	*Digitalis purpurea*								
Hedge Woundwort	*Stachys sylvatica*								
Herb Robert	*Geranium robertianum*								
Marsh Cinquefoil	*Potentilla palustris*								
Marsh Fern	*Thelypteris palustris*								
Marsh Thistle	*Cirsium palustre*								
Tormentil	*Potentilla erecta*								

F. Additional Species Found

Common Name	Scientific Name	O	L	1	2	3	4	5	Note(s) / Photo.

1. Investigating the Landscape: Recording Ancient, Veteran & Worked Trees

INTRODUCTION

There is a variety of species, age of trees and growth forms in the landscape, some of which occur close together in woods, hedges and plantations whilst others are individuals isolated or in scattered groups. It is those trees in the latter groups as well as the big old trees which need to be recorded as they may indicate former wooded areas linked to the history and past management practices. For example, if all the old worked trees are pollards it may indicate that you are in former wood pasture or a deer park. In particular stunted, twisted trees or trees with tangled branches such as 'medusoid' oaks and smaller trees such as Rowan and Hawthorn need to be recorded. These trees may be very old and have easily been overlooked in the past. More information is given about these trees in Section 1 which should be read before carrying out these surveys.

Worked trees have often been managed for centuries before being abandoned as markets and management practices changed. A coppice stool for example, can be extremely old but the stems arising from it can be relatively young. This gives the appearance of a cluster of small-stemmed trees rather than one large tree with a single stem. The size of the individual stems can indicate when the tree was last coppiced so, if practical, individual stems should also be measured.

From the walk-over survey, you should have identified some notable or obvious worked trees to be recorded in more detail. Recording the worked trees can be carried out as a separate excercise or in conjunction with the botanical indicators survey.

THE SURVEY FORM

CONTEXT

Make a note of where the tree is growing and any other features or similar trees growing close by. This will help you to build a picture of the history of the treescape and what has happened within it. Describe if the tree appears to be growing in, on or adjacent to another feature (man-made or natural) and sketch the relationship on the reverse of the survey sheet.

TREE DATA

Where possible identify the species of tree that is being recorded. There are very good guides available, for example, by The Woodland Trust who also now have a tree identification website http://www.british-trees.com/introduction and the Field Studies Council http://www.field-studies-council.org/publications.aspx which you can use. Make a note of which part of the tree you used to identify it, for reference.

Measuring the Girth of a tree

If your tree has a main single stem it should be measured at approximately 1.5m above ground level (known as dbh). Make sure your tape is level around the tree. It is advisable to measure your tree at least twice to check your reading. This is especially the case when the tree is on a slope or amongst boulders. Note the girth in metres or centimetres (e.g. 3.24m or 324 cm). If your tree has a single stem but is burred or knobbly at 1.5m then you can move the tape down the stem to get a more accurate reading. The same is true if your tree forks at or below 1.5m.

If your tree is a coppice stool or other multi-stem you can carry out some extra measurements.

Firstly, measure around the coppice stool at the narrowest point (or around the stems at the narrowest point if no stool is present). This approximates to the girth of the tree. Note at which height you have taken the measurement (below 1.5m). Secondly, count the number of stems and then measure the largest two or three stems at 1.5m above ground level. If you want to measure a multi-trunk, each trunk should be measured separately as you would a coppice. If this is not possible as the trees have merged too high up the stem, measure them as one tree but note that the tree is a multi-trunk and make a record of the number of 'separate' trunks. You can also make a sketch of the tree form.

Tree girth varies with the age of the tree, the species, the growing conditions and past management. The *Ancient Tree Forum* have produced a guide to the approximate sizes and ages of trees but this is not based on upland / poor growing conditions.

Make a record of whether the tree is hollow or partially hollow in the centre. Vertical hollows or splits may be an indication of a lightning strike. It is also useful to record associated features of the tree, for example, smaller cavities, rot holes and burrs on the trunk and associated species growing on the tree such as moss and lichens. These may indicate age, former usage or damage to the tree.

SKETCHES AND PHOTOGRAPHS

An annotated sketch of the form of the tree with notes on where measurements were taken should be included on the survey form as a record of what the tree looked like at the point of survey. If there are any associated features either on the tree or in context it will be useful to sketch these. Similarly a photographic record of the form and type of tree can be compiled and may be used to verify the species.

Measuring an out-grown coppice stool.

1. *Investigating the Landscape: Ancient, Veteran & Worked Trees Survey Form*

1. GENERAL INFORMATION

Site Name		Surveyor(s) Name(s)	
Woodland Area / compartment (if applicable)		Date of Survey	Reference Number (from walk-over)
Grid Reference		Altitude (metres asl)	Aspect (NSEW)

2. CONTEXT INFORMATION (RECORD ALL THAT APPLY / ADD NOTES IF NECESSARY)

Landscape Character close to feature	Woodland Wood Pasture Shrubs/ brambles Felled trees Boulder Slope Boggy / rushy area Other habitat Comments
Topography & Geology close to feature	Steep Undulating Gently Sloping Flat Outcrop rock Stream / wet area Other (describe)
Relationship to other features / or similar trees	Yes / No Number Type Adjacent / Next to/ Parallel Nearby (within 30m) Connected
Chronological evidence (if any)	For example, tree growing in hollow or on top of mound

3. SUMMARY OF TREE DATA

Tree Species		Identification used eg, in leaf, bark, bud, fruit	
Overall Girth of Tree and height recorded at.		Total number of vertical stems.	
Tree Form (see background sheets for details.)	Bundle planting Coppice Stored Coppice Pollard Lapsed/abandoned Pollard Stub Maiden/Standard Medusoid Shredded Phoenix Layering/laid		
Tree Features	Trunk cavities / decay holes Burrs / burls on trunk Dead wood in tree Fungi / Moss / Lichens on tree Other (specify)		

4. SUMMARY SKETCH SHOWING FORM OF TREE

Sketch (overall form) :

Total girth (measure at approx. 1.2m from ground where possible):

Number of vertical stems:

Stem girths (for multi-stem forms):

Maximum:

Minimum:

Maximum internal distance between stems:

Layering / laid length:

Notes:

5. SKETCH(ES) SHOWING TREE FEATURES AND CONTEXT (OPTIONAL)

6. LINKED PHOTOGRAPHS (REFERENCE NUMBER AND DESCRIPTION)

2. Background & Context: The History & Development of Treescapes (Tree'd Landscapes)

INTRODUCTION

A 'shadow' or 'ghost' wood, by definition, is not obvious in the landscape as a typical ancient woodland. Individual trees also appear in the landscape either associated with buildings or boundaries or natural features. These types of landscape can be more usefully thought of as 'Tree'd landscapes' or Treescapes. Woodland blocks can also be included within this definition as may roadside verges as they form part of a landscape which contains trees and indicator plants such as Bluebell. The term Treescapes is becoming more widely used. This section gives definitions of 'shadow' and 'ghost' woods, examples of each of the main types of tree'd landscapes and the sort of treescapes which may contain 'shadows' and 'ghosts' in the project area.

DEFINITIONS

A 'shadow' wood can be described as an area which may contain ground flora associated with ancient woodland and /or a scattered distribution of small veteran or worked trees.

A 'ghost' wood may or may not contain small veteran or worked trees but will have a ground flora associated with ancient woodland.

An 'ancient woodland' is commonly held to be one whose documented history can be traced back to medieval times (prior to 1600). It may be listed on the Ancient Woodland Inventory and given some protection from development.

TYPES OF TREE'D LANDSCAPES OR TREESCAPES

GENERAL

A treescape encompasses all forms and species of tree and shrub, from the ancient oaks in Calke Abbey to the small veteran rowan and hawthorn on the eastern Peak District moors and the ancient holly coppice or field boundary Ash trees in other areas. It will also contain twentieth century blocks of conifer plantations which at a landscape level may disguise the existence of older woodlands. Four broad categories of Treescapes have been identified, by amongst others Oliver Rackham (2003). These can be used to construct a basic landscape typology. This typology is useful in placing 'shadows' and 'ghosts' in context and is set out in the table below.

Table 1: A Typology of Treescapes

Type	Description	Occurence of Trees / Shrubs
Maquis	Heath / moor / bog (low growing shrub layer dominates)	Rare / Occasional
Savanna(h)	Grassland / pasture with a predominantly open canopy interspersed with tree/shrub canopy cover which may be linear (hedge)	Occasional / Frequent
Woodland (ancient coppice-with-standards / managed)	Mixture of open and closed canopy areas with trees and shrubs of varying ages and stages of growth.	Abundant / Dominant.
Forest (in UK contemporary plantation)	Close-grown mostly even-aged trees of same species in a distinct area which are then felled at the same time.	Dominant.

EASTERN PEAK DISTRICT 'SHADOWS' AND 'GHOSTS'

Treescapes of all the broad types outlined in the table above can be found in the eastern Peak District and it is possible to find 'ghosts' woods in maquis, savanna or forest treescapes. 'Shadow' woods are more likely to occur in maquis or savanna treescapes and here they can also be put into four different broad categories within the upland areas which are the main focus of this survey pack. These are as follows:

- Medusoid trees growing in and amongst boulders at the bottom of the Edges or in steep-sided valleys.
- Hanging woods in steep-sided valleys or cloughs.
- Areas of wood pasture (either formerly or currently used) which may now be within enclosed fields, in-bye land or part of a designed parkland landscape.
- isolated or small clumps of scattered small trees on the moor itself.

Medusoid Oak at Gardom's Edge © Paul A. Ardron

Oaks in Yarncliffe Wood © SYBRG 2009

Wood pasture at Longshaw. © SYBRG 2009

Old Hawthorns at Buckstone © Averil Hudson 2012

PERSISTENCE AND CONTINUITY IN THE LANDSCAPE

Since the last ice-age tree cover has fluctuated across the landscape. The first species to colonise were Aspen, Birch and Willow. The latter two remain pioneer species moving onto areas which are no longer grazed or, for example, in former quarry sites. Pine, Hazel, Alder and Oak were the next to become established followed by Elm, Lime, Ash, Beech, Holly, Hornbeam and Maple. Each of the tree species are best suited to particular soil and climate so some never colonised the local area, for example Beech, but have been planted in more recent times.

Natural factors such as underlying geology and soils; climate including sudden severe weather events (floods and fire); and grazing by large herbivores had an impact on the tree cover across the treescape and may continue to do so today. However the largest impact has been the human one. From mesolithic hunter-gatherers onwards trees and woodland cover have been manipulated by humans to provide for their needs.

This led to the growth of a wood-based technology which still persists today although it is not easily recognised because of the legacy and influence of industrialisation and reliance on petro-chemicals. As F.T. Evans (2003) pointed out a wood-based technology meant that there needed to be a varied tree and shrub resource to call on and use, as he said, "An engineer of 1830 would have known the properties of as many as 130 different timbers." This resource had to be protected and managed to make it sustainable at a local level; and, where settlements persisted, the resource may have been looked after over hundreds of years even up to the late twentieth century in some cases.

A useful distinction, especially where 'shadows' and 'ghosts' are concerned is between domestic / local use of tree products and industrial / commercial use. The former includes shelter and fodder for livestock; food, fuel and medicine for humans; materials for the local millwright, cartwright, tanner, blacksmith, farmer and carpenter providing for the village / township's needs. Trees and shrubs such as Hawthorn and Yew were also significant as boundary markers between settlements, waymarkers across the moors and as markers for meeting places. These trees took on a specific meaning for the community, they were protected and often recorded. The local domestic usage may have exploited the smaller fragments of 'hanging' woodland or scattered trees on boulder slopes which today are not recorded as woodland and do not appear in Natural England's Ancient Woodland Inventory. Isolated trees or scattered groups may indicate former farmsteads or be a marker of a former boundary. The persistence of specific species of trees may relate to traditional uses and needs of the local community. For example, Holly was used as winter-feed for livestock, Elder and Rowan were traditionally planted next to farms to keep away disease etc.; Ash, Oak and Elm were needed for building materials.

Industrial / commercial usage is typified by 'simple coppice' or 'coppice with standards' woodland which developed as an income generator for local landowners. In coppice woods the trees were periodically (generally every 10-30 years) cut down to the ground, called a 'stool', from which they grew multiple stems, called coppice or underwood. In a coppice-with-standards, some trees were not coppiced but allowed to grow on to become mature single-stemmed trees, called standards. These were grown to various ages. The coppice provided wood and the standard trees provided timber. Coppice woods were valuable and particularly vulnerable to grazing damage in the first few years after they were coppiced. For this reason, they were surrounded by stock-proof fences, either banks with external ditches or with stone walls. These woodland boundary features often survive and are important archaeological remains which may persist in the landscape when the woodland has gone. Here the tree resource was managed to produce standard products eg charcoal, whitecoal, bark, puncheons and rails for local industries. The landowner may have exploited the resource directly to maintain the estate's industries or let the rights to make and take the products to others under the stewardship of his woodward or land agent. This form of management became more widespread from the sixteenth century onwards and continued until its demise in the later part of the nineteenth century. It is the classic 'ancient woodland' which occurs today, recorded on the Ancient Woodland Inventory. If it was clear-felled and / or replanted in the late nineteenth and twentieth centuries it may persist as a 'shadow' or 'ghost' in the landscape.

The other main and longer-lived traditional type of woodland management is *wood pasture* which occurred in three main forms: Wooded Commons, Royal Forests and their private equivalent Chases, and in Deer Parks. *Wooded Commons* were unfenced areas where commoners (people who held land in the open fields, or were tenants of the manorial lord, and had customary rights) had the right to graze their animals and to take other products such as fuel and building materials. They usually had the rights of cutting underwood, harvesting the wood from pollards, and taking dead wood, but not the right of felling the timber trees. Their common rights were called estovers or botes (e.g. hedgebote, wood for making fences). This typifies the domestic-scale usage mentioned earlier. The tradition often continued until the land was subject to an Enclosure Award but may have persisted later in some areas where customary rights persisted. Evidence of this older landscape can sometimes be found in later planted woodlands as well as in areas which are still used as wood pasture.

A *Royal Forest* (and Chase) did not necessarily mean or imply woodland. Forest here is a legal term for land on which 'Forest Law' applied, relating to the hunting of deer, the grazing of animals, the clearing of land and the felling of timber. Forests and chases were not fenced and could include woodland, heath, moorland, fen, farmland, and settlements and extend for many miles. People living in these areas were able to use tree products for their domestic use governed by Forest Law. In the local area, the High Peak Forest is one example and historically the boundaries of Sherwood Forest also covered part of the area.

Deer parks were private estates of the nobility owned through a grant of land from the crown. Some parks dated back to Anglo-Saxon times. They were enclosed by a stock-proof boundary and had internal boundaries within the park separating different land uses. The parks were multi-functional, used not just for hunting but also to provide food for the lord's table, timber, and even arable crops, fuel wood from pollards, tree fodder, building stone and more. Besides deer which were often carefully farmed, medieval parks contained hares and rabbits (introduced or re-introduced by the Normans), game birds, fish in fishponds, and sometimes wild swine and cattle. Domestic cattle and sheep were also grazed. Although there are records of parks without trees, deer parks usually consisted of large, open-grown trees (mostly Oak), some woodlands protected from grazing, and areas largely cleared of trees (with grass or heath). People worked for the landowner looking after the different functions of the park but weren't necessarily able to take any of the tree products for their own use. Deer parks were at their most abundant in the Medieval period. In the sixteenth and seventeenth centuries, many well-wooded deer parks were converted into compartmented coppice woods, or 'improved' for agriculture as the economic benefits of these forms of management increased.

Current thinking acknowledges the presence of pseudo- or linear woods such as ancient hedges, woodland fragments, and ancient trees from parks and chases. It also reflects the dynamic nature of landscape through time and includes trees planted in post-medieval parks and gardens contributing to our understanding of landowners and landscape designers and woods planted to commemorate famous battles such as Trafalgar. Many woods of more recent vintage also contain historic remains equally diverse, or more so, than of those in older woodlands. Another, often forgotten point is that many 'natural' woodlands develop through ecological successions on post-industrial sites and on abandoned heaths and moors. Some of these are of considerable interest but often generally neglected.

2. *Background & Context: Archaeological Features*

INTRODUCTION

The range and type of archaeological remains and features which can be found associatd with contemporary treescapes may vary with the continuity of woodland cover. It may depend on whether it can be classed as ancient, secondary, re-grown or replanted. The type of woodland, for example upland Oak-Birch wood, or Alder-Willow carr, affects the uses it was put to, its likelihood of being cleared or how it was maintained in the past, and so the types of archaeological evidence which may persist.

Where land has been converted for arable agriculture for example, archaeological features have often been destroyed through ploughing and levelling of the land. This is not the case in areas that have had tree cover for centuries or may not be the case in more marginal upland areas used for grazing. Here features are more likely to survive, both those caused by activities directly associated with woodland management and those that happen to be in the woodland, possibly originating from earlier land-use. In some cases, features may also survive in secondary or more recent woods, but this will depend on past management and levels of disturbance. Understanding this complexity is important if a treescape is to be appreciated in its entirety and to be conserved effectively for the future. Recognition of the evidence and awareness of its potential vulnerability is vital. The existence of a 'shadow' or 'ghost' woodland or even isolated trees within a treescape may be linked to or identified through associated archaeological features.

Remains of a Whitecoal Kiln, note the change in vegetation showing the outline . © SYBRG 2007

Woodland archaeological remains incorporate and survive as:

- soils, sediments, and buried deposits including seeds and other organic material preserved in water-logged ground;
- living and dead trees and their remnants;
- stones, structures and ruins;
- material scattered on site - such as flints, cast off tools and equipment, domestic materials from settlements, etc.;
- earthworks such as banks and ditches, and platforms and pits; and,
- the vegetation itself.

Archaeological features found associated with treescapes may be related to:

- Land ownership and management (banks, ditches, gateposts, hedges, walls, boundary trees).
- Woodland processes and products (pits, platforms, sawpits, storage and processing sites, access routes and trackways; settlement sites).
- Industrial extraction (stone, coal and other minerals) and industrial processes (smelting, milling, production of potash and gunpowder).
- Agricultural phases of land use (field systems, boundaries, buildings, plough marked stones).
- Recreational and sporting activities now (wargaming, pheasant shoots) and in the past (Victorian

pleasure gardens).
- Settlement sites (from prehistoric to modern).
- Military activity (trenches and bolt-holes; bomb craters; tank platforms, searchlight and gun emplacements).
- Transport structures (tramways, packhorse routes, bridges).

PITS AND PLATFORMS

There are many different types of pits and platforms found in treescapes, but not all relate to specific woodland uses. Some may relate to other industrial uses such as mineral extraction; others may be co-incidental, for example, military tank platforms; and others may be natural features. It will probably be difficult to distinguish between some of these without a careful survey and background historical research. The list below gives a description of the more common types of pits and platforms found in or associated with local treescapes.

1. Relating to Woodland Processes
CHARCOAL HEARTH
These are common archaeological features in many local ancient woodlands but may also be found in secondary woods or in the wider treescape if the ground surface has not been greatly disturbed.

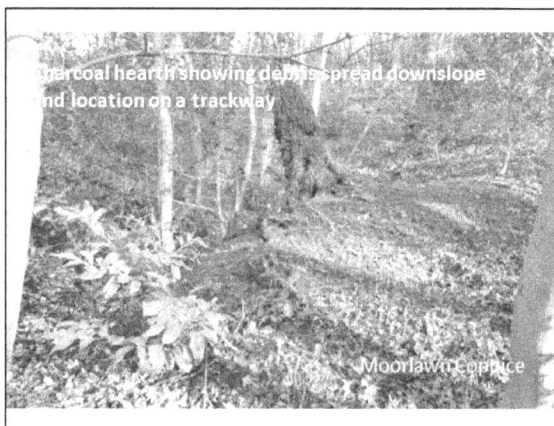

Remains of a Charcoal Hearth. © Paul Smith 2012

- Identification: normally all that now remains is a round shallow depression in the ground (around 5 metres in diameter) or a flat surface cut into a slope with a retaining wall on the down-slope. Fragments of charcoal are sometimes seen within the hearth area as an additional clue.
- Process: a circular stack with a central flue was built from lengths of wood about 1.5m long, cut from coppice poles and covered by turf (to prevent complete combustion). A fire was then set in the central flue which was covered over and sealed leaving the wood inside the stack to smoulder and turn into charcoal (partly combusted wood).
- Associated with the hearth was a larger platform area used by the charcoal collier (burner) as his camp and processing area.

WHITECOAL KILN OR Q-PIT
Today, few whitecoal kilns or Q-pits are well preserved, however the stoke hole can often be distinguished, as can the remains of the stone lining.

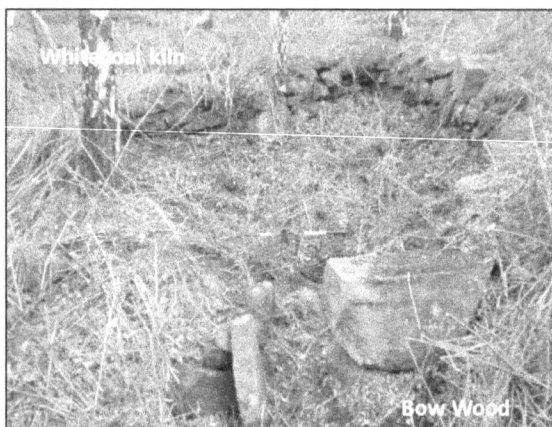

Remains of a Whitecoal Kiln. © Paul Smith 2012

- Identification: a roughly circular shaped hollow in the ground surface (between 1 and 2 metres in diameter of variable depth) with a channel coming off one side of it, known as a 'Q' pit because of this shape.
- Process: These structures were used to produce kiln-dried pieces of wood known as whitecoal. It is understood that small lengths of wood (approx. 0.5m in length) were stacked on stone lintels built

across the hollow, then covered over with turf. A fire was lit underneath the lintels and the channel used as a ventilation shaft to draw the heat through to dry the wood out.
- They are similar in form to Potash kilns and can be confused with these in some areas of the country because they were both stone lined, roughly circular depression.

POTASH KILN

The potash manufacturing process involved two stages: firstly, burning vegetation to ash and secondly, boiling down or 'elying' a solution of water and ash in a large metal cauldron.
- Identification: The main surviving evidence is in the form of circular stone built structures where green vegetation was burnt and the ash collected. Other evidence can be seen in variable and often shallow depressions and pits which may have been where the 'elying' took place or could be the sites of less industrial ash burning.

2. Both Relating to or Incidental to Woodland Management

PROCESSING, STORAGE AND BUILDING PLATFORMS

Individual platforms may be associated with industrial processing in woodlands or be the remains of small farm-steads and shepherd's shelters. A line of small platforms with building material may be old shooting butts or associated with much earlier settlements.

Platform feature © Paul Smith 2012

- Identification: often now seen as areas of levelled ground, rectangular, square or circular in shape lying close to a track or path. They may have some stone or building material associated with them.
- It is useful to note whether they occur singly or in groups and the spacing between them to help understand their origin and context. They may have isolated trees growing alongside them with remains of dry-stone wall enclo-sures and these should also be noted.
- Their age and former use may be difficult to confirm without historical or more detailed archaeologi-cal investigation because of the longevity of settlement and changes across the eastern Peak District.

3. Incidental to Woodland Management

MINES, QUARRYING AND STONE-GETTING PITS

The Sheffield region is rich in minerals which have been exploited for centuries leaving subsequent evidence of mining and quarrying ranging from prehistoric and Roman (such as for quernstone [grindstone] manufacture) to twentieth century building stone.
- Identification: these form a diverse range of features which may vary in size and complexity from hollows a few metres across to large, opencast quarry sites.
- Process: some of the small features may relate to woodland management where the objective of stone extraction was to build a woodland boundary or to construct the features associated with wood-land industries, for example whitecoal or potash kilns. Disused mine entrances, adits and ventilation shafts are sometimes found associated with treescapes. So called 'bell-pits' from earlier surface mining for minerals and stone such as coal or ironstone are distinctive as the spoil from the excavation was deposited round the vertical shaft creating a circular 'donut' mound. The shaft was often loosely back-filled so the middle of the 'donut' may be unstable.
- Many entrances and shafts will have been identified and mapped by the Ordnance Survey with

historic maps showing more details of the mining or quarrying operations. Additional survey may be unnecessary apart from confirming the locations within your overall project.

- Under no circumstances should you enter any mine shaft or tunnel: they can be extremely dangerous.
- Historical research is usually needed to verify the use for the quarried material.

Old quarry site, Yarncliffe Wood © SYBRG 2012

TREE-THROW PITS

When a tree falls over, usually as a result of high winds, it leaves a pit where the root plate once anchored the trunk into the ground, known as a 'tree throw'. These may be quite recent or centuries old.

- Identification: If a tree fall is recent, the presence of the fallen tree, or of an existing stump, will make it easy to distinguish the depression from an artificial earthwork. However, if the stump has rotted away completely, it can be very difficult to confidently interpret the pit that is left. Usually, tree throw pits are approximately circular and about 1 to 4 metres in diameter, depending on the species and size of tree. Sometimes, there are more clues: a semi-circular pit with a mound along its straight edge is characteristic of a fall in which one side of a large root plate has remained partially embedded in the ground, forming the earthen mound after decades of gradual decay.

- Confusingly, some artificial earthworks, such as small-scale quarries and 'weapons pits' dating to the Second World War, can look very similar after seventy years of erosion. In these cases, analysis of the wider distribution pattern and/or reference to historical sources is usually the key to telling the difference.

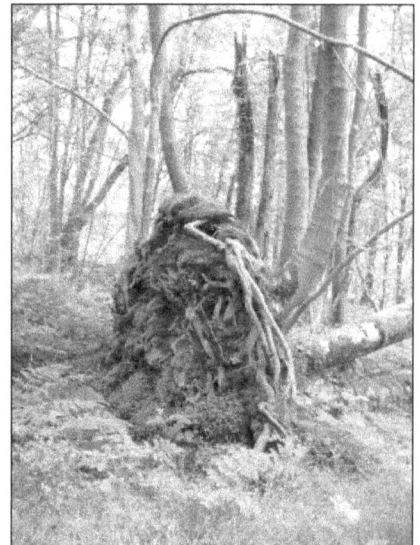

Recent Tree-throw. © SYBRG 2012

LANDSLIPS

The type of treescapes which may contain 'shadows' and 'ghosts' are often found on land that is unsuitable for arable agriculture: on steep slopes, boggy ground, or heavy soil. Clay sub-soils, especially, can combine all three of these factors likely to promote woodland, but they also create conditions under which landslips can occur, especially after wet weather. Therefore, woodland and landslips often coincide.

- These landslips vary in size and can later be confused with artificial platforms or exploratory diggings. As with tree throw holes, the key to dismissing a particular mound or hollow as a natural feature is to be aware of the underlying geology as well as a thorough examination of the surrounding area and referral to historical sources.

- Depending on the geological and other physical conditions these features may also be linear. If this has recently occurred it is usually fairly obvious but if it has happend a long time ago it may mimic a boundary feature.

MILITARY REMAINS

During the twentieth century in particular but also earlier the moorland and woodland areas to the west of Sheffield were used by the army and local defence corps as training grounds, storage areas and defensive sites. In some parts of the area, military remains are abundant, and include pillboxes, weapons pits and slit trenches, concrete bases for buildings, and networks of tracks and areas for storage and vehicle parking. These may since have been re-colonised by trees or contain older trees which have managed to survive the military activity. Medusoid and phoenix trees or remains of trees may also be the result of the military activity. Craters left by bombs may also be found. Some features of military activity such as trenches and platforms may be mistaken for older features associated with former woodland managements so again historical research is important to find out their origins.

LINEAR FEATURES

Linear features can offer remarkable insights into the history of our landscape and are some of the most important historic features you may come across in your research. They may include boundaries and route-ways but also ancient cultivation areas such as field lynchets. Some boundaries are not continuous features on the ground, but are marked at intervals by boundary stones and distinctive immovable landmarks, such as watercourses, natural outcrops, and prehistoric monuments. There are many different types of linear features found in treescapes, but only a few relate specifically to woodland uses. The list below gives some information about the commonest types of linear features.

BANKS

Banks used as an outer boundary of a woodland were usually quite substantially built. They were designed to provide a barrier to prevent uncontrolled grazing and trespass by both grazing animals and humans. These outer woodland boundaries varied in their construction depending on the materials to hand. Often there was a ditch on the outside of the wood and then a bank to stop animals or people getting in. There may also be walls, fences or hedges on the top of the banks to strengthen the defence. These types of boundaries are often a feature of an ancient woodland. Hedges on their own were also used as a barrier around the edge of a woodland.

Remains of a substantial pre-enclosure wall in Bow Wood - possibly associated with a quarry
© Paul Smith 2012

- Identification: banks may still be apparent as a boundary feature around a woodland today if the extent of the woodland has not changed. Where there have been changes the bank may now exist within the woodland, be some way outside the woodland (and much less obvious) or no longer be continuous. Comparison with old maps and estate documents will assist in working out whether the boundary was an external one.
- Woodland managed on rotational coppice was often divided into compartments by less substantial banks and ditches so that animals could graze in some areas but be excluded from others. These may also still occur and can be traced inside a wood.
- Other banks may occur within the woodland associated with trackways, settlements, mining and quarrying or industrial processes. These features may be relatively recent or be centuries old. They may indicate that the woodland was cleared at some time in the past or is secondary and has grown

up more recently over an older landscape. Consulting old maps and other documents will be necessary to find out what the banks were used for.

HEDGES

Hedges or a row of out-grown enclosure hawthorn trees, for example, may occur within a woodland, around the edge of a woodland or separately. These may indicate that the woodland or part of the woodland is more recent; the hedge may have once surrounded a garden and dwelling or workshop/industrial complex or it may be along the line of a field boundary. In some cases there may be a scatter of older trees such as out-grown pollards within the area enclosed by the hedge which may be an indication of an area of former wooded common or wood pasture.

Out-grown Hawthorn hedge on Burbage showing evidence of laying © SYBRG 2009

- In the upland areas where dry-stone walls are more prevalent there may only be remnants of hedges perhaps created at the time of the Enclosure Awards but then abandoned as land-use changed. Old hawthorns spaced out in straight lines which show signs of having been layed are evidence of these.
- First or Second edition Ordnance Survey maps are good places to start to look for old field boundaries and hedges as one of their functions in the nineteenth century was to accurately survey boundaries of landownership so lines of individual trees were recorded across a landscape.

TRACKS AND ROUTEWAYS

Trackways, in particular, can reflect the history of a piece of woodland and persist in a wider treescape even though their function has been lost.

- Trackways across areas typified by deeply eroded 'hollow ways' (trackways used heavily and thus eroded to form a sunken path) are largely the product of industries or centuries of transport by pack animals. In this area along the eastern Peak District what are now often braided hollow-ways were used by pack-horse trains in medieval times.
- Trackways can also include rides, carriage drives and avenues, linked to aristocratic traffic or with the many minor houses and halls that dotted the landscape during the eighteenth and nineteenth centuries, and may also be related to farmsteads.

Hawthorn by old track at Longshaw © SYBRG 2012

- Trees may still mark some of the routes, planted along them in Victorian times or been used as markers across the open moorland areas in historic times.
- Tramways associated with mining and quarrying activity may also be found. Similar to trackways they lead to the site of the industry but will probably be more substantially built and on a shallower incline. It is worth noting that both physically and over time many of these features had multiple and over-laying uses.

2. *Background & Context: Botanical Indicator Species*

Introduction

Plants in general have specific requirements in terms of growing medium, pH, moisture, light, slope, climate and altitude (Ellenberg Values). They and their allies, fungi, may all be classed as 'indicators' of a particular set of growing conditions and specific habitat-types, e.g woodland or wetland; areas with high nutrient levels etc. Some have very precise requirements others are more general and able to grow in a range of habitats e.g common nettle. The distribution of plants is influenced naturally by different mechanisms used in reproduction, e.g. wind-blown seeds, creeping rhizomes and by grazing as well as by human influence. All these factors come into play when considering 'indicator species'. This section focusses specifically on indicator species related to wooded areas.

Botanical Indicators of Ancient Woodland

Lists

Work has been carried out over the last thirty years and more, and is still ongoing, on developing lists of species which have strong associations with known ancient woodlands and can therefore be used as indicators. Woodlands are classed as ancient using the accepted definition 'in existence prior to 1600' although it is important to remember that almost all the woodlands will have been managed in some way since then altering the ground flora in some way. Important attributes for a woodland indicator are its tolerance to shade, its potential to colonise new areas and resilience to grazing or other disturbance. In general the lists relate to the ground flora component of the woodland but may, as in the case with the list used in the survey form, also include trees and shrubs. Lists for specific regions have been developed to reflect different growing conditions and historical management across the UK. They are still subject to refinement as further data is gathered and interpreted alongside historical and archaeological studies. The list used in the survey form has been derived from a list initially put together for the Peak District by Penny Anderson and Peak Park NPA ecologists in the 1970s. This refined list groups species according to 'strength of association' with ancient woodland rather than treating them equally as indicator species.

In the case of 'shadow' and 'ghost' woodlands the list of local ancient woodland indicator species is used to identify what may once have been a wooded or more heavily wooded landscape. If several of the 'strongly associated' species occur together then this may indicate a site of a former ancient woodland which may be confirmed by historical research.

Depending on habitat-type, aspect and geographic location, many woodland plants can survive away from a continual or cyclical tree canopy and so persist as a 'ghost' wood. This may be due to factors such as shade from rocks, abundant water or bracken cover mimicking the tree canopy. These areas may not be heavily grazed allowing plants intolerant of grazing to survive. Species such as wood sorrel may persist in grazed areas by growing within and amongst hollow stems of trees. Excluding animals from formerly heavily grazed areas often allows species such as bluebell to re-emerge.

Shadow ancient woods may occur in some plantations, secondary woodlands or ornamental planting schemes which had previously been cleared. These areas may be overlooked because of their present management regime but may exhibit continuity with an older landscape. Other shadow woods, part of the wider treescape, may have a mixture of a few worked trees across an area together with some ground flora indicators. These may be in steep sided valleys or at the bottom of the Edges and boulder slopes not recorded as woodland or managed in any way.

SPECIES

The full list of species used is given on the survey form (see pages 19-21). A few of the more common examples are given below.

Strong Ancient Woodland Indicators.

Old Hawthorn with Wood Sorrel growing in the centre. © SYBRG 2012

Bluebell. © Ian D. Rotherham 2012

Common Cow-wheat. © Barry Wright 2012

Wild Garlic (Ramsons). © Barry Wright 2012

Good Ancient Woodland Indicators.

Wild Strawberry. © Barry Wright 2012

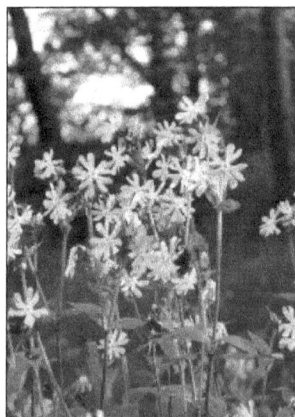

Red Campion. © Ian D. Rotherham 2012

Woodland Indicators

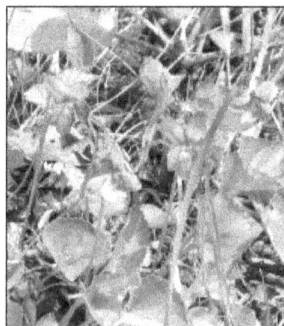

Common Dog Violet. © Christine Handley 2012

Crab Apple. © SYBRG 2012

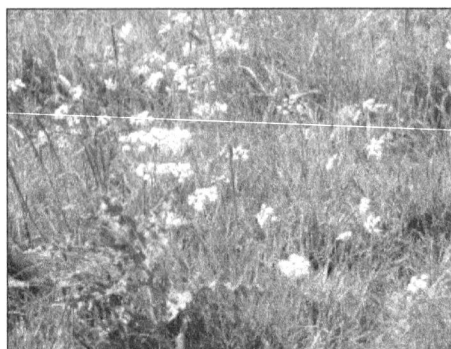

Pignut. © Christine Handley 2011

Possible Indicators

Marsh Marigold © Christine Handley 2011

Associated Species

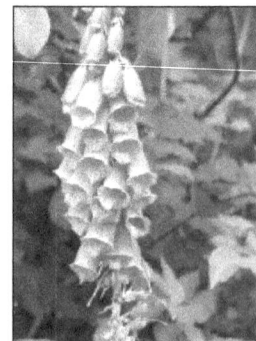

Foxglove © Christine Handley 2011

WAXCAPS AND WOOD PASTURE

Wood pasture is a particular form of treescape with widely spaced trees showing a characteristic browse-line and/or trees managed as pollards (cut above the height of grazing animals). These pasture areas may be part of the historic landscape dating back to pre-enclosure of common land or remnants of a privately owned deer-park. They will not have the same ground flora as an ancient woodland because of their purpose and subsequent management. Instead, they will have their own distinctive suite of species adapted to the conditions.

Wood-Pasture at Longshaw. © SYBRG 2012

These species include the waxcap fungi (*Hygrocybe* genus), fairy clubs (*Clavariaceae*), earth tongues (*Geoglossaceae*) and Entolomas all of which are particularly associated with long-established grazed grasslands. These grasslands have not been 'improved' i.e. reseeded or artificially fertilised and ploughed up so a range of these types of fungi are able to persist. A few of the very common waxcaps may be found in some grasslands which have been improved. Other fungi, such as those associated with animal dung, can occur in grazed-grasslands. However, it is the range of the specialist species in places such as the Longshaw estate which suggests the continuity of a historical wood-pasture treescape.

Some of the Species Associated with Wood-Pasture

Entoloma incanum © Paul A.Ardron

Parrot Waxcap. Hygrocybe psitticina © Paul A.Ardron

Pink Waxcap. Hygrocybe caliptriformis © Paul A.Ardron

Greying Waxcap. Hygrocybe laeta © Paul A.Ardron

Blackening Waxcap. Hygrocybe conica © Paul A.Ardron

Meadow Waxcap. Hygrocybe pratensis © Paul A.Ardron

Examples of the Trees Recorded During the 2012 Project.

Hawthorn at Buckstone, Derbyshire.
© Averil Hudson 2012.

Alder in Shillito Woods, Derbyshire.
© Sheila Routledge 2012.

Phoenix Birch at Longshaw, Derbyshire.
© Christine Handley 2012.

Phoenix Rowan on Big Moor, Derbyshire.
© Andy Alder 2012.

2. Background & Context: Ancient, Veteran and Worked Trees - species, forms and uses

INTRODUCTION

A tree or shrub usually passes through four life-stages unless it becomes diseased, damaged or is harvested as a timber tree. These stages of growth, maturity, decline and decay have been described for the oak by Ted Green as 'from acorn to ancient'. The sketch below (figure 1) taken from Ted's paper in *Medieval Parks and Parklands* illustrates the growth and decay pattern of an open-grown oak. Similar growth patterns and sequential changes can be constructed for other species and for those grown in dense woodland conditions (another example from his paper of a forest-grown tree is given in figure 2.)

Figure 1. Sequential changes to the deadwood and hollowing of an individual open grown oak "A supply of successional, structural, sustainable decaying wood from acorn to ancient" © E.E.Green

Figure 2. Sequential changes of the canopy area and trunk girth of forest form trees. Overall time span in the case of oak could be less than 400 years and in the case of beech between 200-300 years. © E.E.Green

Ancient, veteran and worked trees may be the most visible parts of a Shadow or Ghost wood. They are indicators that a tree'd landscape has persisted and trees have been used by humans over a long period of time. The terms ancient and veteran are sometimes used interchangeably and both can describe worked trees. Ancient trees usually exhibit veteran characteristics but veteran trees may not be especially ancient in absolute terms. Different tree species grow at different rates and reach their 'ancient' phase of life at different times. The lifespan of a tree is usually measured for an open-grown standard tree growing in good soil and climatic conditions. Managing or modifying the form of a tree on a cyclical basis as a 'worked' tree can prolong its life. Definitions of the terms ancient, veteran and worked are given below.

Ancient

An ancient tree is one that is classed as 'very' old and in the declining (end) stage of its life; normally such trees have a larger girth than other trees of the same species. The term describes trees defined by three guiding principles:

* trees of interest biologically, aesthetically or culturally because of their age;
* trees in the ancient (final) stage of their life; and
* trees that are old relative to others of the same species.

Ancient trees will almost certainly exhibit some of the micro-habitat characteristics which are associated with veteran trees.

Ancient oak (over 800 yrs old) at Calke Abbey, Derbyshire.
© SYBRG 2005

Veteran

A veteran tree is usually in the mature stage of its life with micro-habitat features including; hollowing, holes, wounds and large dead branches. Veteran trees may also be of interest for cultural, historical or aesthetic reasons.

Worked

A worked tree is one that has been managed by humans to generate wood, worked timber or tree fodder for a particular usage e.g. charcoal making, for firewood and/or building materials. Coppice and pollards are common forms of worked trees. These trees are often very old but may look younger because they do not exhibit the classic characteristics of an ancient or veteran tree.

Veteran oak in Sherwood Forest with microhabitats and dead wood.
© SYBRG 2005

In many cases worked trees were managed for centuries before being abandoned around the beginning of the twentieth century as the demand for locally sourced wood-based products declined. In a few areas trees continued to be worked until the 1970s and more recently there has been a revival in these traditions. Some abandoned worked trees were felled and removed when woodlands were converted to plantations but there are still many abandoned worked trees which survive today. They can give an insight into the history of the surrounding landscape.

TREE FORMS

Coppice

The stem of a tree is cut at ground level to encourage growth of multiple stems from the base (known as a stool). These stems (known as poles) are then cut back at periodic intervals which may be as little as just a few years or up to thirty years depending on the variety of purposes they may be put to. This was a very common form of management for trees over several hundreds of years. The coppice tradition had largely died out by the early twentieth century but many coppice stools and the outgrown stems survive. They can often now appear as circular clumps of quite large trees with the original base having decayed to form a hollow (see right hand picture).

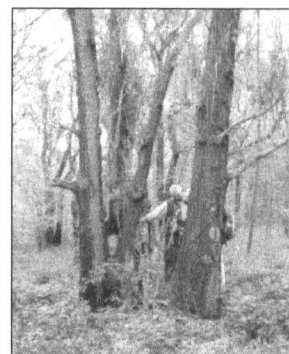

Recent coppice (left) and outgrown coppice (right) .
© SYBRG 2010

Stored Coppice

The creation of this form often occured when the coppicing tradition was abandoned. One or two stems were selected from a large coppice stool to continue to grow as standard timber trees. This has sometimes resulted in what is known as an 'elephant's foot' at the base of the tree.

Layering

This can take place naturally as part of phoenix regeneration when a branch or fallen tree takes root. It is more commonly seen in old hedges where humans have exploited the natural process and have 'laid' the hedge to create a dense stock-proof barrier then the management of the hedge has lapsed. The re-growth after layering grows vertically up towards the sun creating a character-istic pattern of growth.

Old laid hedge © SYBRG 2006

Natural 'layering' from fallen tree.© SYBRG 2007

Maiden / Standard

A tree that has been grown in its natural form as a single stem for timber production in a woodland or as an open-grown tree outside woodland.

Medusoid growing amongst rocks. © SYBRG 2011

Medusoid/ Corkscrew

These trees are often found in upland rocky areas as irregu-larly shaped multi-trunked / multi-boughed trees. They are characterised by their sprawling growth forms in and amongst the rocks. They may have been used in a similar way to coppice and pollards or have grown naturally in response to grazing and climatic conditions. They may be of considerable age.

Open-grown misshapen tree. © SYBRG 2010

Open-grown (distorted / misshapen)

This form occurs when the tree has been subject to either ad-verse weather conditions causing the main trunk and branches to grow at an odd angle or become misshapen. Pressure from a heavy snow fall may also cause the tree to take on a collapsed appearance. In addition the tree may be exposed to grazing on its higher branches which distorts the form of the tree. Some sessile oak trees (*Quercus petraea*) appear to have a natural corkscrew form in upland areas.

Phoenix Regeneration

This occurs when a tree partially or completely collapses to the ground. The tree then roots from the sides of the main trunk or large branches which are touching the ground creating a new tree or a series of trees.

Lime showing natural 'phoenix' regeneration.© SYBRG 2005

Pollard

A tree whose stem has been cut above the height of grazing animals' browse lines to create a number of stems (known as poles). The pollarded tree is then managed in a similar way to that of a coppice stool. Pollards were created in areas of wood pasture, for example in deer parks and on commons.

Lapsed/Abandoned Pollard

These trees result from the abandonment of the pollarding tradition. If they now occur in a woodland this indicates that the area was formerly much more open and grazed by large herbivores. Due to the smaller stems being cut

Out-grown pollard
© SYBRG 2011

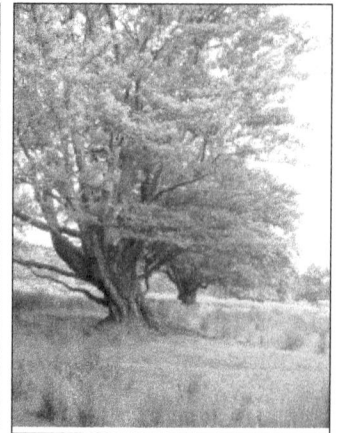

Short/ stub-pollarded beech.
© SYBRG 2012

repeatedly to encourage new growth from the main trunk, a lapsed pollard has a short trunk with a mass of vertical 'branches' above it. These may look natural, however if they all come from the top of a trunk at about the same height it could be an indication of an abandoned pollard tree.

Stub/Short Pollard

This type of tree has a main stem or trunk that was cut in the past above coppice (ground level) but lower than pollard (grazing animal) height. As with coppice and pollard, smaller stems grow from the cut stem. These had similar functions and their management was also abandoned.

Shredded Tree

This form occurs when the side branches are repeatedly removed from a tree trunk, often for animal fodder. The harvesting of the branches creates small groups of thin stems growing laterally from the trunk of the tree instead of large branches.

TREE & SHRUB SPECIES AND THEIR USES

The trees and shrubs listed in the table relate to the most common ones found in the local area. It is not a comprehensive list of those found more generally.

Trees	Shrubs
Oak (*Quercus* spp.)	Hazel (*Corylus avellana*)
Ash (*Fraxinus excelsior*)	Holly (*Ilex aquifolium*)
Elm (*Ulnus* spp.)	Rowan (*Sorbus aucuparia*)
Birch (*Betula* spp.)	Elder (*Sambucus niger*)
Alder (*Alnus glutinosa*)	Hawthorn (*Crataegus monogyna*)
Willow (*Salix* spp.)	Juniper (*Juniperus communis*)
Crab Apple (*Malus sylvestris*)	
Field Maple (*Acer campestre*)	
Sycamore (*Acer pseudoplatanus*)	
Beech (*Fagus sylvatica*)	
Sweet Chestnut (*Castanea sativa*)	
Lime (*Tilia* spp.)	
Yew (*Taxus baccata*)	

COMMON USES OF TREES AND SHRUBS AND THEIR PRODUCTS

Alder: Clog-making and for charcoal which was used for making gunpowder.

Ash: Waggon building, wheel rims, hay rakes, ladder-poles, tool handles and police truncheons.

Beech: Furniture making, ladder rungs, rolling pins, tent pegs, treen and ox yokes.

Birch: Various uses including spoons and dishes; textile industry (bobbins, reels and spools); besom brushes and bundles made from twigs were used to take impurities from molten steel; sap used for wine and 'sugar'; bark for making baskets; firewood.

Crab Apple: food; shelter; treen

Elder: berries and flowers for food and medicinal purposes; insect repellent; protection against evil spirits

Elm: Used for furniture; for water pipes, piling under bridges and keels of wooden ships; chopping blocks and wheel hubs.

Hawthorn: Used for hedging (layered); boundary marker; human and animal food.

Hazel: Hurdle and basket making; fish traps; hoops for barrels; thatching spars; shepherds' crooks; and nuts.

Holly: Winter animal fodder; bark used for bird lime; butter prints and engravers' blocks; and horse whips.

Oak: Beams and posts for house and ship building; tree nails and ship pins; wheel spokes; furniture; mining pit props; fencing; coppice poles for charcoal; bark used in tanning industry; acorns used for pannage (pig fodder).

Rowan (Mountain Ash): tool handles; fruit for jam-making; deliberately planted for warding off evil spirits.

Sweet Chestnut: Used in furniture making; for pit props; charcoal and a source of tan-bark.

Field Maple and Sycamore: Used for kitchen and dairy utensils; rollers including washing mangles; wood-turning, carving and musical instruments).

Willow (Osier): Used in basket making; for tool handles; flooring of carts and barrows; and milkmaids' yokes.

Yew: Used for bows and by the Vikings to produce nails. Often boundary and churchyard trees.

FLEAK HURDLES—CORD-WOOD—CHARCOAL. 235

siderable scale, from underwood Poles and thinnings of Plantations: he saws down the Poles by circular Saws, instead of cleaving and chopping them, and bores the mortising holes by Centre-bits turned by the Mill: this practice might be advantageously adopted in other situations, and by which the Poles would be all carried out of the Spring Woods to be manufactured, as I have recommended.

Turnip-fleaks, with four bars and two yards long, of cleaved Oak, hooped at top, and pointed for driving, are sold about Lullington at 5*s*. or 5*s*. 6*d*. each.

I shall, perhaps, not have a more fit opportunity than this to mention, that at Mr. Samuel Tudor's at Cox-bench, and Mr. Richard Harrison's at Ash, I saw a new sort of *Fleak Hurdles, made of Cast Iron,* four feet high, with five light yet strong ribbed bars, two yards long, with dove-tails at top and bottom of the heads, by which these Fleaks are effectually locked together, as they are set, and to iron Stancheons pointed for driving into the ground: these Fleaks were cast at Bridgenorth in Shropshire, by Messrs. Hezledine and Rastrick, and cost 9*s*. each delivered at Stourport (whence they came by the Canals): Fleaks of similar form but of less dimensions, for Sheep, 7*s*. each.

Cord-wood, of round Billets from refuse underwood and lop, 11*s*. per cord of 128 cubic feet stackt.

Charcoal, is made in considerable quantities in Sir Thomas Windsor Hunloke's Spring Woods in Win-gerworth, the refuse Underwood from the Puncheons, &c. and lop of the Trees, being first cut and stackt in Cords, each eight feet long, four wide, and near five feet high (in order to allow for hollowness, four feet being considered the standard), and containing about 155 cubic

Copy of Page From General View of the Agriculture of Derbyshire by John Farey, 1817. © Michael Parker 2012

3. *Using and Interpreting the Findings*

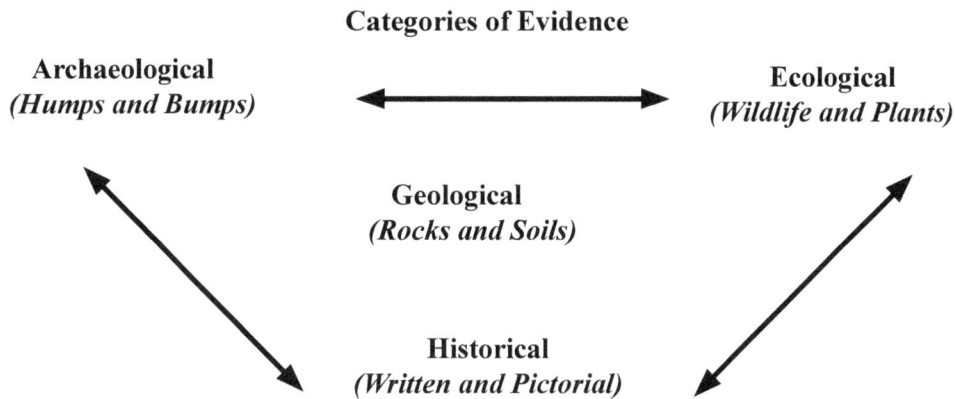

Categories of Evidence

Archaeological
(Humps and Bumps)

Ecological
(Wildlife and Plants)

Geological
(Rocks and Soils)

Historical
(Written and Pictorial)

INTRODUCTION

Individual surveys of sites for archaeological, ecological or geological features are valuable as a starting point to understand the development of a treescape. However, bringing together different types of survey evidence and then carrying out historical research enables a fuller and more detailed picture to emerge. Sites where documentary and landscape evidence can be integrated are more valuable still and can provide a biography of the treescape over several centuries. This helps to identify the different phases and uses the treescape has undergone, the legacy of these in the landscape and sets a specific location within a wider social and economic context.

The following kinds of information can emerge from the documentary study of a treescape:

*   Status or designation of the treescape and changes in ownership. (Is it or should it be classified as 'ancient'?).
*   The significance of boundaries and internal earthworks. (Are they related to management of the treescape or of a non-woodland phase?)
*   Woodland clearance(s) and woodland extension(s). (Has the shape and function of the wood changed?)
*   Past management practices (Was it a wood pasture, simple coppice or coppice-with-standards, plantation or a product of natural regeneration and domestic use?)
*   Clarification of the status of different tree and shrub species (Are they 'exotic' species for the area i.e not naturally occuring in a specific location; has any planting taken place and of what species?).
*   Markets for the wood, timber and other woodland products. (Who used them, what were they used for, when and where?).
*   Other land-uses of parts of the treescape. (Is there evidence for quarrying or mining; mill sites; leisure (grouse-shooting / gardens); settlements?)
*   The relationship of trackways, routeways and settlements around and through the treescape. (Are they related to woodland management practices or incidental to these?)

PLANNING THE DOCUMENTARY RESEARCH

It is worth contacting the landowner to ask about management operations which may impact on the surveys (and get permission if necessary) and if historical research is planned as they should have details of where the estate archives are held. Below are some basic steps to help provide a structure for conducting the research project. It is important to plan the research carefully and think about the key questions that need to be answered due to the wide range of sources and limited amounts of resources which may be available to carry out the work.

Some of the key questions to address are:
*   When was the treescape first recorded? (including place-name and field boundary evidence)
*   Who were or still are the local owners? When did they change?
*   How was the treescape managed in the past? Has it been continuous or changes in uses?
*   Are there records of clearance or planting? If so, what and when?
*   Are there any records of woodland crafts eg besom making carried on in the area?
*   What industries are recorded locally? What use did these make of wood products?

Decide on the amount of time which can be spent on documentary research and what the budget might be. Depending on the location of the sources of information, there may be travel costs and, or costs for making copies of the material if this is allowed.

It is useful to look on a modern map and note the nearest village(s) / settlements and any place names or prominent features which are in the area as a starting point. These will help when looking through references, indexes and carrying out archival searches. Note should also be taken of landowners and any changes in place-names when earlier maps and documents are found. Sometimes items are listed with alternative spellings in indexes so some detective work may be needed to locate documents etc.

Books including local histories and guidebooks may give sources of information which can be used as a starting point. These may be found in the local branch library which may also have its own lo-cal studies reference section. Many now also have computers with internet connections or connections to on-line library catalogues which can be used for preliminary work. Choose a couple of types of informa-tion to focus on initially. Maps are an easy starting point as the series of Ordnance Survey maps go back to the mid-nineteenth century. Enclosure Award and Tithe maps may be available as may maps made for land surveys of estates or when railways, roads and canals were built.

Once the preliminary work has been done, plan the visit to a library, archive centre, SMR or even a more systematic trawl of the internet using the keywords and questions devised earlier. Opening times will vary and sometimes appointments are necessary to consult some material. Record offices have membership requirements so you will need to enrol on your first visit. There will be rules or restric-tions on what can be brought with you and how you can view and handle some of the material. Specific instructions and opening times can usually be found on their websites or by phoning or writing to them. There may also be a facility for pre-ordering material so that it is available to look at when you arrive.

Although this may seem obvious it is important especially if there are a few people carrying out the reserach to decide on a filing system and an index to cross-reference to the site survey evidence at the beginning of the project. The findings from the different surveys and documentary research need to be regularly reviewed so that gaps or apparent dead-ends or new avenues in the information can be assessed. This is better than being confronted with a large pile of material which is difficult to manage. It is also advisable to put a time limit on the research and move to the report writing, interpretation and analysis stage quite quickly. This will help to keep things 'fresh' and help form the next set of research questions or decide on other lines of enquiry.

Finally try to stay focused on addressing your initial set of questions but note any points of inter-est, potential areas for future investigation as you go along.

USING THE INFORMATION

The first stage in using the information from documentary research and survey work is to collate the data and make an assessment of its reliability. This means looking at all the evidence gathered in a critical way, perhaps discarding some and putting a question mark against others for further investigation. It is good practice to get into the habit of doing this at an early stage, as is reviewing the information when new material comes to light.

There will be a high degree of reliability in surveys where factual measurements and basic descriptions are involved. Where features are being interpreted initial reliability may be less without background work. Documentary and historical records will also need to be interpreted cautiously. These were created for a particular purpose and with a meaning and significance which may not now be apparent. As already mentioned it is better to use different types of evidence to corroborate details rather than rely on a single source. In cases where there is only one source, a further judgement will need to be made on what weight is given to the evidence it provides.

The next stage is to look at all the data from your sources (survey and documentary) for each of the research questions. One useful way of doing this is to create a table or matrix for the evidence. This can be compiled as data becomes available as it will provide a useful summary of how the different sources fit together and enable links to be made between different surveys and documents. It will also show up gaps in information and perhaps suggest new links which are not immediately apparent. This process is key to understanding and interpreting the data from the surveys and placing the findings in context. It should also pick up anomalies or isolated pieces of information which may need further investigation. The aim, by the end of the process, is to have several different types of data (survey and documentary) which suggest a single interpretation which can be independently verified. Background reading from standard texts will help with suggesting possible interpretations. A list of these for the subject area is given in the bibliography.

Once the collation and review process has been carried out, the findings need to be written up into a report. This can be a simple summary of the findings covering a few pages with perhaps a map and a couple of illustrations or it can be a detailed report with measured plans and recommendations for management. The purpose of the report and its intended primary audience should guide the outcome. It is better to produce a series of short reports on particular topics or areas of a treescape than try to produce a large report covering every aspect. The report may include all of the following sections but should include those marked with an asterisk (*) as a minimum:

- How the research was carried out, who by and when*
- Purpose of the research and the key questions covered.
- Background to the treescape (location, size, topography, geology, ownership)*
- Summary of the historical research*
- Summary of the field surveys*
- Analysis and interpretation of the findings
- Summary of main points and suggestions for further research work*
- Recommendations for management work
- References and Bibliography*
- Appendices (including copies of survey forms)*

DEPOSITING THE SURVEY INFORMATION

It is important that a copy of the information gathered through surveys and research is given to any funders of the work and to the landowner for their records. In the case of work carried out in this area the Peak District National Park Authority should also be sent a copy of the report. This should make the landowner aware of any areas of the treescape which are significant in terms of archaeology and/or ecology and may need to be taken into account in future management plans. With the owner's permission, a copy of the information should also be given to relevant organisations so that a permanent public record is made. Doing this will mean that this work in turn becomes part of the future historical record which others can use. Often people are happy to receive electronic copies of reports which cuts down costs and storage.

The County Archaeology Service which maintains the Historical Environment Records / Sites and Monuments Records should be sent a copy of the report and survey sheets relating to the archaeological features for their records. This is important so that the service has an accurate picture of known features and finds within an area as they are one of the central reference point for planning and other enquiries. The service should be consulted at the beginning of the work to find out what is already known about the area. The 2012 project area was covered by the Peak District National Park Authority which also maintains its own Historic Environment Records and copies of surveys were deposited there.

Similarly, if any ecological records have been made, the Biological Records Centre (BRC) or Local Authority Ecology Unit or Museums Service should be sent a copy of the surveys and report for their records. Local natural history groups may also have recording schemes which link to the BRC and these in turn link to national recording networks such as the NBN. Extracts of records for the local area can also be obtained from the national networks via the internet.

There is a national recording scheme for notable, ancient and veteran trees, *the Ancient Tree Hunt* hosted by the Woodland Trust. Records of these trees have been added onto their website by members of the public. Details of the trees are available using their interactive map which can be downloaded from their website. New records are continually being added and if you find any potential trees it is worth adding these to their database which covers the UK. At present many of the trees are the classic large open-grown veterans of parkland. The type of trees which may be recorded during the 'shadows' and 'ghosts' project have often been overlooked in the past so now need to be added to the database for future reference.

The Local Studies section of the library may be happy to receive a copy of the report or a summary of the information for their files. Other local groups in the area may also be interested in receiving a copy and may have other information to share which is triggered by the information supplied.

Information from the report can be used in other ways. A summary can be posted onto a website or blog with accompanying pictures. Extracts from the report can be turned into a leaflet, poster or booklet perhaps targetted at different audiences. Public walks can also be organised to take people to some of the features mentioned in the report.

The main message from this section is, unless there is some constraint on making the information public, findings from the research need to be distributed and used. In this way the findings contribute to the on-going debates about the evolution of these treescapes, their current and future management, and highlighting their importance.

4. *Glossary of Terms*

A

Ancient Semi-natural Woodland: ancient woodland sites that have retained the native tree and shrub cover that have not been replanted. They may have been managed by coppicing or felling and allowed to regenerate naturally.

Ancient Tree: a tree that is very old and in the declining (end) stage of life; normally such trees have a larger girth than other trees of the same species. The term encompasses trees defined by three guiding principles: 1. trees of interest biologically, aesthetically or culturally because of their age, 2. trees in the ancient stage of their life and 3. trees that are old relative to others of the same species.

Ancient Woodland: woodland that has been under continuous tree cover from 1600AD. Then ancient woodland can be primary woodland, Ancient Semi-natural or Ancient replanted.

Ancient Woodland Indicators: species which because of their characteristics (shade tolerance, slow colonisation and restriction to woodland habitats) tend to be found in old established woodlands. These are most commonly vascular plants (flowering plants and ferns) or Ancient Woodland Vascular Plants (AWVPs).

Archaeological Remains: buildings, earthworks, artefacts (including ecofacts such as veteran trees and hedges), subsurface deposits and environmental data.

B

Beech Mast: the prickly fruits of beech trees which contain the beech nuts used as fodder for pigs.

Bell Pit: a hollow created by shallow mining using an unsupported vertical shaft sunk into the ground.

Berl: mark made on a tree (by the head woodman) to denote whether it is to be retained or cut down.

Besom: broom with bunches of twigs (often birch) for the head; used both domestically and industrially.

Black-bark: a timber tree which has grown through two coppice cycles (between 40 & 50 years old).

Bloomery: a type of furnace once widely used for smelting iron.

Bole: 1. main trunk of a pollard or 2. early lead smelting site often situated on a hilltop; remembered in the place name 'bolehill'.

Bolling: the trunk or stem of a tree; and may also be used to describe the trunk and cut branches of a pollarded tree.

Bote: denotes the rights of commoners to gather wood or timber for particular purposes on common land, e.g. cart-bote, house-bote, hedge-bote.

Brash: small branches trimmed from the side of a tree; a process known as shredding.

Broadleaved Woodland: woodland where the canopy has less than 10% of coniferous trees.

Bundle Planting: when several tree seeds are planted in the same hole, and multiple stems arise (a common feature of historic parks and gardens).

C

Canopy: the layer formed by the leaves of trees which form the highest vertical layer in a woodland.

Carr: ancient Norse name for wet woodland.

Charcoal: a carbon containing material made by heating wood or other organic matter in the absence of air.

Charcoal Hearth: the area used to process wood into charcoal. Often all that remains is a round shallow depression in the ground or a flat surface and retaining wall cut into a slope.

Chase or Frith: a private hunting area, which may be forested or open.

Clough or Ghyll: term used for a narrow wooded valley in northern England.

Coke: mineral coal from which most of the gases have been removed by heating.

Common(s): a piece of land over which people exercised traditional rights, such as grazing their animals, collecting timber etc.

Compartment: a subdivision of woodland, historically an area of land used for forest inventory and/or management.

Conifer Woodland: is woodland where the canopy has 10% or less of broadleaved trees.

Coopering: making or repairing wooden casks.

Coppice Ring: an old coppiced tree where the middle of the coppice stool has died and new shoots grow from the stump forming a ring of shoots.

Coppice: technically a tree whose trunk has been cut close to the ground to encourage growth of young poles (shoots or suckers) which can be harvested.The term is also used to describe a dense stand of scrub.

Coppice-with-standards: an area of woodland where most of the trees are coppiced but a few are allowed to grow into timber trees.

Cordwood: wood cut into four foot lengths and then stacked in piles eight foot long, four foot wide and four foot high which makes a load of about two tons.

Cruck: a pair of curved timbers used to support the walls and roofs of houses.

D, E

Deer Park: an area of land enclosed to provide a constant supply of deer and other animals for hunting and food. These areas were also managed for timber and woodland resources.

Designed Landscape: any land purposely planned by humans including parks and gardens.

Earth-fast: objects (for example boulders) held in the ground and not easily moveable.

Earthwork: any artificial feature surviving as humps and bumps visible on the ground surface.

Ellenberg Values: scores given to a plant species in terms of five environmental variables (light, moisture, pH, salt, and soil nitrogen) to indicate the conditions under which that species is usually found - for more details see http://internt.nhm.ac.uk/eb/ellenberg.dsml?button=0.

Enclosure: the conversion of common land into individual ownership, may involve the construction of barriers such as banks, ditches, walls and hedges.

Epicormic Growth: thin, twiggy shoots growing directly from a tree trunk, often forms substantial clumps.

Exotic: an alien species, in this context, introduced from outside Great Britain e.g. *Rhododendron ponticum*.

F

Fall: The verb 'to fall' was used to describe trees that were to be felled. The noun 'fall' was the South Yorkshire word used to describe a compartment within a large coppice wood. The word was also used to describe the felling of underwood and timber in a particular place or during a particular period.

Faggot: bundlesof brushwood tied up with twisted bands (called withies) of ash, birch, hazel or willow. Faggots were used as fuel in bread ovens and for strengthening river banks.

Field Layer: an intermediate layer of vegetation in a woodland, consisting of small non-woody herbaceous plants eg bluebells, daffodils, ferns, the layer lies between the ground layer and scrub / canopy layers.

Flush: either the sprouting of new leaves, or an area where water has washed over the surface or through the soil creating a small area of wetter habitat.

Forest: nowadays a term used to mean a woodland, historically it applied more broadly to any land on which forest laws applied. Forest laws were medieval laws introduced into England by the Normans and designed to protect wild animals for hunting by the aristocracy.

G

Ganister: a type of sandstone with a very high silica content and which was used to make bricks to line blast furnaces.

Ghosts: in this context, the marks left in a landscape by previous woodlands and users of the area.

Goit (also leat / lete or race): an artifical water channel that connected water-powered industrial sites to the rivers or streams on which they were located. The head goit is a water channel leading to a water-powered wheel and the tail goit, a water channel leading away from the wheel.

Ground Layer: the lowest plant layer of a woodland, up to 10 cm above the ground and consisting of mosses, lichens, small flowering plants and seedlings.

H

Habitat: a particular type of local environment, the place an animal or plant lives.

Hammer Pond: pond used for providing power to water-powered forges.

Herb Layer: layer comprised of ferns, grasses, flowering and non-woody plants between the ground and shrub layers in a woodland.

High Forest: woodland dominated by tall trees (standards) suitable for timber.

Historic Environment: all the physical evidence for past human activity and its associations that people can see, feel, find and understand in the present world.

Hollin, Holling or Holly Hagg: an area where holly was historically managed to provide leaf fodder.

Hurdle: a small gate made of woven wood, used in temporary animal shelters.

I, J, K

Ironstone: a sedimentary fine-grained rock, important as a source of iron (iron ore).

Keystone species: a species that has a key role in an ecosystem.

Kid(d): a bundle of small branches and twigs of wood; similar to a faggot but smaller.

L

Landslip: downhill movement of unstable earth and rock, etc.

Lapsed pollard/coppice: a pollarded or coppiced tree that has not been cut for many years.

Laund or plain: an open area of land containing mainly grassland and scattered trees usually found in parkland, see also plain.

Layering: when part of a tree (branch or trunk) is bent or falls into the horizontal and shoots grow from this upwards towards the sun. This may occur artificially as seen in a layered hedge or naturally if a tree or branch falls over.

Leaf fodder: cut leafy branches of trees cut to provide grazing for domestic animals.

Lording: a timber tree more than fifty years old.

M, N, O

Maiden: a tree that has never been cut and thus has a single main stem.

Medusoid: a tree with a convoluted and sprawling appearance often growing amongst boulders

Mixed woodland: where the canopy is comprised of 10% or more of both Broadleaved and Conifer trees.

Multi-trunk: a tree which has several trunks growing up together which may occur naturally. Multi-trunks may look similar to a coppiced tree.

Newcastle rail: length of wood used for wooden railway tracks.

Old growth: a tree which has not been managed for over 200 years.

Orchard: a plantation of fruit / nut trees.

Ornamental tree: a general term referring to a tree bred or grown for the beauty of its structure, foliage and flowers rather than its functional reasons.

P, Q

Pale: a high fence or wall often surrounding a wood or deer park.

Pannage: autumn feed for pigs in woodland (for example beech mast or acorns), or a payment for pasturing pigs in woodland.

Park: land containing widely spaced trees and enclosed for domestic or wild animals.

Pen pond: small pond lying close to a larger pond, used to fill the main pond during dry weather.

pH: a measure of acidity and alkalinity on a scale of 0 to 14, where a PH of 7 is neutral, a pH of less than 7 is acidic and a pH of greater than 7 is alkali.

Pitstead: another name for a charcoal hearth (from northern England).

Plantation: a woodland where most of the trees have been deliberately planted for timber production.

Pole: a young tree or a stem from a coppice or pollard, of a size suitable for making poles.

Pollard: a tree whose trunk has been cut at 2 to 4 metres above the ground, i.e. above the height of grazing animals, then allowed to regrow to provide a crop of young branches, (see also bolling.).

Potash: describes any material containing potassium, but is specifically used to describe potassium carbonate (lye) mixed with other potassium salts derived from wood ashes. Potash was used in dyeing, soap and glass manufacture and as a fertiliser.

Processing platform: levelled areas, cleared of smaller trees and undergrowth lying close to a road or path within a woodland, used to store wood and timber products from woodland industries.

Q-pit: a Q shaped hollow in the ground surface, linked to the historical production of whitecoal.

R

Ramel / Rammel(l): first recorded in fifteenth century woodland records in South Yorkshire in Latin as *ramayllis*. It means brushwood and was used to make faggots. Rammel is now the South Yorkshire dialect word for rubbish.

Remnant trunk: stem of a tree where the inner part of the wood has been lost through decay leaving the whole or part of the outer stem (living part of the tree).

Ride: These are sometimes called Ridings in South Yorkshire. A ride was and still is constructed to provide access for the extraction of wood, timber and bark, fire fighting, inspection and setting out of coppice-with-standards. As well as being used for sport and recreation by their owners.

Ridge and Furrow: a term used to describe the pattern of peaks and troughs created in a field from a system of ploughing with oxen from the Middle Ages.

Royal Forest: land over which certain rights were reserved for the monarch and /or aristocracy. It was introduced to England by the Normans in the eleventh century; at its height one third of the country was designated as Royal Forest.

S

Saw pit: a rectangular hole in the ground used to saw tree trunks into planks by two people, one working above the hole and the other in the pit.

Scrub layer: a layer of woody vegetation (shrubs and seedlings / saplings) lying beneath the main tree canopy of a woodland, but above the ground and field layers.

Secondary woodland: woodland that now grows on land that, at some time in the past, was cleared of trees and used as pasture, meadow, arable.

Shred or shredding: the process where side branches are removed from a tree often for use as fodder.

Shrub Layer: layer of small trees and woody plants between the herb layer and canopy.

Smelting: the process for extracting metal from ores.

Spring: a term used to describe a coppice-with-standards woodland in the West Riding of Yorkshire and Derbyshire.

Standard: a tall straight tree with a trunk of 1.8 metres or more which is suitable for use as timber.

Stool: the base of a tree left after coppicing.

Stub or Stubbin: a. the stump of a tree, the piece remaining on a trunk or branch after it has been cut. b. a short pollard, where the tree has been coppiced above ground level but below the level needed to protect the re-growth from grazing animals, often found in ornamental planting.

T

Tanning: the process for preserving animal hide as leather by primarily using extracts of tannins from tree (especially Oak) bark.

Tar: a viscous black liquid derived from the distillation of organic matter, including wood.

Timber: large trunks of trees which are suitable to be sawn into planks (lumber).

Tithe: a tax or assessment of one tenth of produce levied on all communities to support the established church.

Topography: the shape of the land.

Trackway: a beaten or trodden path, sometimes deeply eroded by use to form a hollow way.

Tree throw: the blowing over of a tree by strong winds, this may leave a small hollow in the soil which when the tree has rotted away may be mistaken for a pit.

Turf: the surface layer of soil containing a mat of grass and grass roots.

Turnery: the use of a lathe to turn solid wood into shapes for chair legs, pegs, toys, etc.

U, V

Understorey: the plants growing under the main canopy of a woodland.

Underwood: the lower storey of a woodland (lying under the canopy layer of trees) and/or of coppice/pollard poles or suckers.

Vera Hypothesis: the theory that the original woodland cover (the Wildwood) did not consist simply of dense woodland, but was made up of a patchwork of woodlands, open grassland and solitary trees, before human modification.

Veteran tree: a tree that is usually in the mature stage of its life with micro-habitat features including; hollowing, holes, wounds and large dead branches. Veteran trees may also be of interest for cultural, historical or aesthetic reasons.

W, X, Y, Z

Waver: a young maiden tree that had only grown through one coppice cycle.

Whitecoal: kiln-dried wood used as fuel in lead smelting.

Wood: a term used to describe branches of a tree which are smaller than timber, or to describe an area covered in a dense canopy of trees. Coppicing produces wood not timber.

Wood pasture: a very open type of woodland, a cross between grassland and woodland, historically often used for grazing.

Woodbank: an earthen bank often topped with trees, a stone wall or laid hedge.

Wooded landscape: a generic term for woodland, parkland, wood pasture, former forest and other trees-capes.

Working or Worked tree: a tree which at some stage in its life is or was managed by humans to generate wood for a particular purpose, such trees normally have a modified shape/form.

Field Visit to Blackamoor © SYBRG 2012

5. Bibliography.

Anon. *Tree I.D: Ancient Tree Guides.* Woodland Trust (free to download).

Anon. (2004) *With alidade and tape.* English Heritage free guidance publication.

Anon. (2007) *Understanding Archaeological Landscapes: a Guide to Good Recording Practice.* English Heritage (free to download).

ArcHeritage (2011) *Eastern Moors Estate Historic Landscape Survey Report.* Eastern Moors Partnership.

Ardron, P.A. and Rotherham, I.D. (1999) Types of charcoal hearth and the impact of charcoal and white-coal production on woodland vegetation. *Peak District Journal of Natural History and Archaeology*, **1**, 35-47.

Barnett, J. and Smith, K. (2004) *The Peak District Landscape through Time.* Landmark Publishing, Ashbourne.

Bevan, B. (2006) *From Cairns to Craters: Conservation Heritage Assessment of Burbage.* Moors for the Future Report No.8, Peak District National Park Authority.

Bevan, B. (2007) *Sheffield's Golden Frame: the moorland heritage of Burbage, Houndkirk and Longshaw.* Sigma Books, Berkshire.

Bowden, M. (2000) *Furness Iron - the physical remains of the iron industries of Furness and Southern Lakeland.* 1st Edition. English Heritage.

Bristow, J. (2001) *The Local Historian's Glossary of Words and Terms.* Countryside Books, Newbury.

Caunce, S. (1994) *Oral History and the Local Historian.* Longman.

Dymond, D. (1999) *Researching and Writing History: a Practical Guide for Local Historians.* British Association for Local History, Salisbury.

Evans, F.T. (2003) The Age of Wood In Rotherham I.D., Jones M. and Handley, C. (eds.) *Working and Walking in the Footsteps of Ghosts Volume 1: the Wooded Landscape.* Wildtrack Publishing, Sheffield

Gelling, M. and Cole, A. (2000) *Landscape of Place-names.* Martin Tyas.

Green, E.E. (2007) Stating the Obvious: the Biodiversity of an Open Grown Tree - from Acorn to Ancient In Rotherham, I.D. (ed) The History, Ecology and Archaeology of Medieval Parks and Parklands, *Journal of Landscape Archaeology and Ecology*, **6**, 48-52.

Griffith, G.W., Bratton, J.H. and Easton, G. (2004) Charismatic Meta-fungi the conservation of waxcap grasslands, *British Wildlife*, **15(3)**, 31-43.

Jones, M. (2009) *Sheffield's Woodland Heritage* (4th Ed.). Wildtrack Publishing, Sheffield.

Jones, M. (2013) *Gapping, Raddling and Snagging*. Wildtrack Publishing, Sheffield.

Kelley, D.W. (1986) *Charcoal and Charcoal Burning*. Shire Publications Ltd., Oxford.

Muir, R. (2005) *Ancient Trees, Living Landscapes*. Tempus Publishing, Stroud.

Peterken, G.F. (2000) Identifying ancient woodlands using vascular plant indicators, *British Wildlife*, **11**, 153-158.

Preston, C.D., Pearman, D.A. and Dines, T.D. (2002) *New Atlas of the British & Irish Flora*. Oxford University Press, Oxford.

Rackham, O. (2007) *Woodlands*. Collins (New Naturalist series), London.

Rose, F. (1999) Indicators of Ancient Woodlands, *British Wildlife*, **10**, 241-251.

Rotherham, I.D. (2007) The implications of perceptions and cultural knowledge loss for the management of wooded landscapes: a UK case-study. *Forest Ecology and Management*, **249**, 100-115.

Rotherham, I.D. (2011a) *Animals, Man & Treescapes – perceptions of the past in the present*. In: Rotherham, I.D. & Handley, C. (eds) (2011) *Animals, Man and Treescapes*. Wildtrack Publishing, Sheffield, 1-32.

Rotherham, I.D. (2011b) *A Landscape History Approach to the Assessment of Ancient Woodlands*. In: Wallace, E.B. (ed.) *Woodlands: Ecology, Management and Conservation*. Nova Science Publishers Inc., USA, 161-184.

Rotherham, I.D. (2012) *Traditional Woodland Management: the Implications of Cultural Severance and Knowledge Loss*. In: Rotherham, I.D., Jones, M. & Handley, C. (eds) (2012) *Working & Walking in the Footsteps of Ghosts. Volume 1: the Wooded Landscape*. Wildtrack Publishing, Sheffield, 223-264.

Rotherham, I.D. (2013) *Ancient Woodland: History, Industry and Crafts*. Shire Publications, Oxford.

Rotherham, I.D., Jones, M., Smith, L. and Handley, C. (eds.) (2008) *The Woodland Heritage Manual* Wildtrack Publishing (free version to download).

Rotherham, I.D. and Wright, B. (2011) Assessing woodland history and management using vascular plant indicators. *Aspects of Applied Biology*, **108**, 105-112.

Rotherham, I.D., Handley, C., Agnoletti, M. and Samojlik, T. (eds) (2012) *Trees Beyond the Wood: an exploration of concepts of woods, forests and trees*. Wildtrack Publishing, Sheffield.

Rotherham, I.D. (ed.) (2013) *Cultural Severance and the Environment: The Ending of Traditional and Customary Practice on Commons and Landscapes Managed in Common*. Springer, Dordrecht.

Rotherham, I.D. (ed.) (2013) *Trees, Forested Landscapes and Grazing Animals: A European Perspective on Woodlands and Grazed Treescapes*. EARTHSCAN, London.

Stokes, A. (1999) *Health and Safety Overview*. BTCV.

Tabor, R. (1994) *Traditional Woodland Crafts*. Batsford, London.

Useful Websites

www.ukeconet.org

Ancient Tree Hunt

http://www.ancient-tree-hunt.org.uk/recording

Archives and Local Studies Services

http://www.nationalarchives.gov.uk/
http://www.derbyshire.gov.uk/leisure/record_office/
https://www.sheffield.gov.uk/libraries/archives-and-local-studies.html
http://www.archives.wyjs.org.uk/

British Association of Local Historians

http://www.balh.co.uk/index.php

Council for British Archaeology

http://www.britarch.ac.uk/

English Heritage

http://www.english-heritage.org.uk/
http://www.heritagegateway.org.uk/Gateway/
http://www.heritagegateway.org.uk/gateway/chr/default.aspx

Family / People History

http://www.findmypast.co.uk/home.jsp

Institute of Historical Research

http://www.history.ac.uk/

Maps

http://www.old-maps.co.uk/index.html
http://getamap.ordnancesurvey.co.uk/getamap/frames.htm
http://www.multimap.com/
http://www.google.co.uk/

Museum of English Rural Life

http://www.reading.ac.uk/merl/

Natural England

http://www.naturalengland.org.uk/publications/

Peak Distict National Park Authority

http://www.peakdistrict.gov.uk/looking-after/culturalheritage
http://www.peakdistrict.gov.uk/looking-after/landscape
http://www.peakdistrict.gov.uk/looking-after/biodiversity

Woodland Trust (identification guides)

http://www.woodlandtrust.org.uk/en/learning-kids/Pages/children.aspx

Volunteer Field Visit at Longshaw 2012 © SYBRG 2012.

The survey guide was written and designed by Christine Handley (South Yorkshire Biodiversity Research Group), Professors Ian D. Rotherham and Melvyn Jones (Sheffield Hallam University) and Andy Alder (Nottingham Trent University), Dr Paul Ardron, Paul Smith, Ondrej Vild, Barry Wright and workshop volunteers.

The 2012 project was funded by the Peak District National Park Authority's Sustainable Development Fund.

A version of the guide is available free to be shared but please acknowledge the source if you use it for your own project. Survey form pages from the survey guide may be photocopied. Visit our website www.ukeconet.org and look in community projects.

www.ingramcontent.com/pod-product-compliance
Lightning Source LLC
Chambersburg PA
CBHW081201270326
41930CB00014B/3256

9781904098515